WITHDRAWN
FROM COLLECTION

The Couple

D0862013

WESLEYAN POETRY

OTHER WESLEYAN TITLES BY MARK RUDMAN

Provoked in Venice (1999)

Millennium Hotel (1996)

Realm of Unknowing (1995)

Rider (1994)

ALSO BY MARK RUDMAN

By Contraries

The Nowhere Steps

Robert Lowell: An Introduction to the Poetry

Diverse Voices: Essays on Poets and Poetry

Square of Angels: The Selected Poems of Bohdan Antonych
(with Bohdan Boychuk)

Memories of Love: The Selected Poems of Bohdan Boychuk

My Sister—Life and *The Highest Sickness, poems by Boris Pasternak*
(with Bohdan Boychuk)

Euripides' Daughters of Troy (with Katharine Washburn)

WITHDRAWN
FROM COLLECTION

The Couple

MARK RUDMAN

❧

Wesleyan University Press

MIDDLETOWN, CONNECTICUT

811.54
R916c
c.1

Published by Wesleyan University Press, Middletown, CT 06459

© 2002 by Mark Rudman

All rights reserved

Printed in the United States of America

5 4 3 2 1

CIP data appear at the end of the book

Grateful acknowledgment is hereby made to the journals in which many of the poems in this book first appeared.

Arion: "Perseus Surprised, Andromeda Unbound," "Deceptive Practicality," The Change Seminars," "Hidden Clauses in the Lottery You Can Enter For Free," "Return of the Soldier"; *Boulevard:* from "Fragile Craft": "There is no end to the torment . . ." (2), "I abhor assumptions . . ." (3), "Regret" (4), "Limited Run" (5), "Poolside II: Erratic Behavior" (11), "Direct Hit" (12), "The Tall Woman Appears" (13), "Volcanic Changes in the Paradigm" (15), "Her Generation" (23), "The Killing Sweepstakes" (24); *Drunken Boat:* " Long-Stemmed Rose"; *The London Review of Books:* "Provo," from "Fragile Craft": "The Pretend and the Fake" (18); *New England Review:* "The Guitar Lesson," "The Secretary of Liquor"; *The New Republic:* "Bicoastal: Bobby Darin at the Copa"; *Pequod:* "Positioning in Time," "The Age of Who: Famous Photograph" (1), "Again I was Wrong" (6), "The 'Real' Custer, and in Cinerama Too" (19), "Nakedness Her Shield" (25), "Showing Up Isn't 90% of It for Everyone" (26), *Salt:* "The Shallowness of the Lake"; *Threepenny Review:* "Where the Story Leaves Off"; *Washington Square:* from "Fragile Craft": "The Professional" (8), "Why in the First Place" (10), "Long-fingered Pianist" (20), "Where's Beetlenut?" (21), "The Fuse of Catastrophe" (27), "No Quarter" (28), "Money"; *Yellow Silk:* "The Couple"

"Bobby Darin at the Copa," *To Stanley Kunitz, With Love,* edited by Stanley Moss, Sheep Meadow Press, 2002.

I would also like to thank my friends Karen Bender, Forrest Gander, Charlie Smith, Claudia Rankine, and Nora Sayre (1932–2001) for their varied contributions.

What I like to do: remain lucid in ecstasy.

—ALBERT CAMUS

For Madelaine

For Madeleine

Contents

The Couple

The Couple

PROVO

It's hard to get anywhere in Utah without going through Provo.
I can't tell you the number of times
I went there as a teenager, the number
Of times I drove into town in the early
Afternoon, hungry, and had to look around
For a place to eat. You don't have to starve
In Provo but you eat at your own risk.
At no risk. I would never have gone to Provo
On my own. I went accompanied—
For reasons almost too trivial—or personal—to mention.

There are moments when you simply must get into the car and drive
And from Salt Lake there are only a few ways to go,
Toward the Great Salt Lake or toward the canyons and to get
To Zion or Moab you had to pass through Provo.

I remember the population because it went
With the number of miles from outskirt to outskirt,
45 miles, 45,000 people, 45 minutes
(Keeping to the speed limit)
$45 to spend on a suit at a 45% discount . . .

There was nothing Provo's department store did not carry,
Including pearl handled Colt 45's,
But for a wider selection of fire arms, rifles
With narrowing focal points, with greater precision over vast
    distances,
You were better off
Next door.

O I guess it wasn't that different from entering
A thousand other American towns, but this one
Made my flesh crawl. I wanted to howl.

The men walked with their hands deep in their pockets.
The women were afraid to lift their eyes.
It was as if something terrible had happened
Or was about to happen.

I'm not saying you have to love what you do
In this life, but it isn't nice to practice
The silent treatment on strangers in the desert,
Strangers who would have to be wondering
Where the other 44,990 people were, since
Other than the one drowning potatoes in burning oil

Beside the grill in the luncheonette
And the one behind the register,
And the three grim-faced, parchment-skinned
Jack Mormons hunkered over cups,
And the handful of impassive faces
Placed against the windows
Of one-story cinder-block houses,

There was no one in Provo beyond the jackrabbits—
Glimpsed in abundance en route—
Who vanished as we crossed the town line,
And drove past the population sign.

Or was it a warning in disguise?

There was something eerie in the air,

An absence I could not identify.

An immense single-pump gas station,
Shimmering like a mirage in the heat,
Took up a good part of the main drag.
I pull in. Step into the heat stunned.
The car is too hot to touch.
I needed gas but didn't want to get it there.
It meant digging up the attendant.

You know the lights in hospital corridors.
Those are the lights in the gas station in Provo.
They're the kind of lights that show up whatever's wrong with a face;
The kind of lights that make something wrong when there's nothing
    wrong.

When I got there, I was afraid. It's hard
To put my finger on the precise reason why.
It's not as though something ominous rose
From the sidewalks or Hell's Angels cycles
Were parked outside the luncheonette.
Nothing like that.

Nor can I say why, even though there was almost
No one on the street, I felt watched.

While I slept fitfully in the tilt-back bucket seats,
Someone scribbled obscenities on the headlights.

I felt drawn by destiny to this nadir.

You don't want to provoke anyone in Provo.
It's that kind of place, that kind of absence—

The desert flattens out, the plants
Draw in their antennae.

Provo is not where you can hope to find
Boon companions. It's against the law
To serve liquor in the bar
And no one in the luncheonette looks up
When you walk in.

These are the fallen,
Sunk in ashes, adrift
In the smoke of unreason.

They have masturbated without shame.
They have coveted, envied.
They have pocketed the tithe.

It's hard to put it into words: Provo.
It's more like a place without a name,
A desert stopover with the semblance of a town.

Provo is a place where there is no reason to be.
A province that would never grow up to be a suburb,
Like the backwaters where they exiled
Ovid and Pascal.
Only there is no water—
Just landscape shorn of green and tawny desert colors.
Burned skyline.
Hills like craggy impenetrable fortresses.
The rain gutters hiss in the dryness.
There's a menacing blue tint on the rims
Of impinging mountains.

LONG-STEMMED ROSE

When she says her love is dead
You think she needs you
—LENNON-MCCARTNEY

1

Regrets Only

You didn't have to go.

She pressed me.

You didn't have to go.

She had a way of regressing,
of randomly becoming very needy . . .

And you wanted her to need you.

Like a hook in the jaw.

She had on an extra long
blue nightshirt with the sleeves
pulled up when she asked me.

Lovely blond down on her forearms.

*And by complying with her request
there was a slender chance
that she'd want to see more of you.*

I should have said no.
Not only no, I should have insisted
she shouldn't do it—.

It wasn't worthy of her.

(Pause.)

How could she have fallen for a set-up like that?

And why didn't she call it off when the "couple"
brought another couple?

Outrageous.

Beyond psychology.

Beyond meaning.

No, embedded.

She had a job; she wasn't really hot
for a modeling career.

It was—barter.

This photographer would shoot her unclothed
in exchange for a portfolio
which she could show to agencies.

In other words, there was an element of sense.

I can't remember if he was a legitimate
photographer or cunning amateur.
And the "one roll" metamorphosed.
And it was not he in any case
who creeped me quite as much
as his somewhat butch, domineering wife.

As if she and not he was the secret engine?

Whose job it was—

Whose pleasure—

to hand Laura a long-stemmed rose

while the men were reloading

and she was standing there on the stage
naked, and trembling, like a faun,
and

you wanted to interfere

and also let these creatures, I mean
characters, play out their hand,
see just how far they would go—

you who liked to see Laura's body
whenever it was vestment-free were now revolted
by these lusterless, dour, middle-aged voyeurs
who looked to her for rejuvenation—

That faun-like quality—this side of anorexic—
yet a grown woman, lissome, tall.

Something deceptive about her slenderness
left you unprepared for the fullness of her sex and breasts.

Her body? What about her innocence?

That to her credit was never an issue.

Not with you. But the photographers didn't know
she'd had more sex-partners than you'd had fantasies
peopled with women you'd known.

And she only two years older.

You don't think these hungry-eyed characters
knew that behind her body's lie,
the fake demure virginal shy exterior,
lay a woman who when at all pressed to have sex

"by a fool such as" you, *reported the thousand*
"fucks" she'd undergone in a voice that
bristled with irritation.

She had no room for a slightly

immeasurably

younger and less experienced person's avid interest.

At least when I was that person.

2

It's not that easy, at 21, to gauge how desperate
people more than twice your age can be
for a new sensation; how bored,
how hollowed out and jaded they have become.

The couples pretended to be matter-of-fact.
That this was business.

How?

By assuming expressions of no expression.

Like hit men. *And* women.

Still, when the other couple appeared
Laura could *have relented.*

I pressed her not to go through with it.

And she looked at you, dewy-eyed, as if to say,
"it stinks, but you'll protect me and make sure
things don't get out of hand."

Was she that desperate for a free portfolio?

I can't imagine why when as I said she had no intention of
becoming a model, only of modeling.

For three hours of work she'd earn
what she earned in a week.

Or so she claimed.

She was an immensely practical person.

Or—intensely?

This is standard issue stuff.

The girl whom they entice.
The pressure toward nakedness.

The tapping of her
insecurities, the fantasies

that exceed anything
the offer can offer,

even a spread in Vogue; *a poster hung*
in every bus shelter: a career.

I wish you hadn't brought it up.
Now there's no escape
from the heat of the September night

the vanished summer's stale, pent-up air

rising tormentingly off the tar,

the grainy wooden table in the dim Irish bar
west of 6th on West 4th.

And she rarely wore her hair pulled back

to adopt a clean-cut, fresh-faced look

as she did that night as she ordered a Beck's,
reaching across to rub your knuckles;
intimate, yet not quite coming on.

And all to get me to come along so she wouldn't be alone
in a situation whose outcome she couldn't predict.

I'm not saying that the role of protector didn't appeal.

Or that there might be some reward—even though you'd called it quits.

The part that made me sick was the obligatory dinner,
"our treat," at a generic Beer & Burger joint,
"super-convenient," a mere fall
from the studio.

No one forced either of you to go.
You could have insisted.

I tried! But she was gripped by a notorious
hunger fit and, having to "eat right away what does it matter
who with and why not take advantage of it being free."

And so we went.

Vicious red seats flooded with infrared.
Snow-cone margaritas:
guaranteed blast-off from the high
sugar-content.

"I only drink with friends," I wish I'd had the nerve to say.

(Anyone with any sense had switched to seltzer, soda, beer
or stayed with water, cool and clear.)

But it was good that the uninvited couple
disappeared after the shooting.
Quick good-byes, fast handshakes,
straight delivery: "Thanks for letting us come."

I squelched my reply.

Were they hurrying home to the darkroom?

3

Long-Stemmed Rose

How do you know that the revulsion and contempt
that possessed you during the shoot
wasn't pure, undiluted jealousy: not
wanting to share Laura with the others . . . ?

I don't. I think it was the—transparently fake—way

(while the two gray-haired factotums
were unloading roll one)

                             the wife walked
down the empty aisle at a stately pace,
brandishing a long-stemmed rose,
which she handed to Laura

who appeared to think it was a gift,
and not a fetish-object to add spice
to Act Two when she again disrobed . . . ;

and not as something she was meant to hold
to contrast with her stark nakedness
on stage

when they threw a switch and the kliegs
illuminated her alone on the proscenium.

They wanted to throw more light on the matter.

I asked about the tacky purple backdrop.

They patronized my question by answering with shrugs.

Like "bug-off" kid.

I kept my   jacket on   (collar

up) and crouched in the rear
of the auditorium, gnawing
on my anger.

4

*I have a question. Did she disguise herself to you
any more than she disguised herself to herself?*

Yes, and I would guess that these nudes
were restricted to semi-private use.

I don't recall asking . . .

It was as much the way she opened and slid off
the black and gold silk robe as her eventual nakedness.

Nakedness is after all a fact.

And for those of us who have enjoyed *or endured*
"living conditions amidst the opposite sex from coed dorms to
   retreats to conferences,"
nakedness itself is no aphrodisiac.

Although it *can be . . .*

*What about the photos the master of Nantucket
light took while his wife lay sleeping
naked on the sheet in the summer heat?*

They're hot.

Hot because she'd just been fucked or was about to be?

Hot—because—of heat.

But I never saw any portfolio with head-shots or shots
where Laura wriggled on a stool in clothes
that showed her off to her best advantage.

5

(Someone Must Have Done Something)

There was a history to all this.
Had she given you what you wanted,
were you not still burning from her refusals,
reeling from supernumerous unnecessary hurts
you might have given her this. Been more
companionable. Had she not kept her distance
while you entered the mystic waterfall at Jalapa
alone, had she not chosen to be sick

—clutching her stomach—the same desperate-dramatic
way she did the afternoon we met
only with different   expressive designs

(no mention of hunger   menstrual cramps   P.M.S.)

the morning you were set to go to Teotihuacán

you might have talked to yourself the way they advise
in the self-help pop-psych

books which I railed against

without having read them! I'm not implying that your bias
against behaviorism isn't warranted, but there are
times in men's lives when practicable solutions
are practical.

Not another word about solutions, if you don't
mind, including one I don't think you of all people
need to be reminded of.

"What, moody?"

Is't not my right, my lord? I'm not asking you to disappear so I can
    return to the love . . . ,
the damaged affair I have long felt compelled to examine before
other cares and phantoms crowd in, and crowd out this curious
evanescent moment I have longèd long to reconsider.

I will do what you ask.

It's one thing to say it.

But now as a sprite, a spirit; prisoner of the afterlife;
I can do, or undo, things which gravity, that hanger-on,
makes of life-on-earth a physical comedy for all
concerned—during their tenuous tenure.

Don't fret, I'll be off before you can recite your mother's names.

Nine, not including her given name. Isn't there some
cabalistic significance to the number nine?

Now you're provoking a detour.
And seven and twelve are far more . . .

Propitious?

Expedient. The great wheel needs all twelve spokes to complete its
    revolutions.

Otherwise the months themselves would fall out
like fallout.

I vacillate incessantly between torpor and activity,
numb to anything in between
beyond pure function.

Like obtaining milk for your son.

You've been dead a while now—.

So substitute his current needs and desires
and don't give the little Rabbi a hard time.

(Pause.)

I didn't mean to—

Drop it! Express your thoughts in actions.
And go back to the . . . painful subject . . . of . . .
you and that . . . later Laura—

(after the song, after your laughter in the rain
that wasn't falling with the Laura you really fell for,
after the incident in the bedroom when your mother walked in),

who has risen for
reasons beyond your ken, if not beyond—

❧

Not wanting to be interminably absent with her not well, I abjured
public transportation and let the hotel hook me up with one of those

fly-by-eternity-guided-schleps in a coal-black, battered Pontiac
squeezed between four middle-aged suburban women
in matching polyester schemes that glowed

blinked telegraphed disaster

who had only one question which they repeated
and repeated in a kind of choral fugue:

Is that where the sacrifices were?

Is that where they slit the throats of the children?

I got off one cosmological question
regarding the   placement   of the pyramids
and the number of narrow steps—
52—leading to the Aztec launching pad.

For you—a springboard into eternity;
for others—a chopping block.

So, you were not only inexcusably ignorant
about the Aztec calendar—even for a twenty-one
year old pip fresh out of
(coughs) . . . *excuse me* . . . *if you could call it* (coughs up phlegm) . . .
    that—

I thought you'd eased up on the stogies.

What, you think death is a free ride?
You think I'm coughing for what I'm doing now?

How in hell should I know?

Because I've been—and yes you're right
I've got a sarcastic grin on my face—
instructing you (wasting my breath once more)
in the variance between life before and after.

Maybe one of your friends, like that . . .
that painter born in the camps who wanted you to see
her painting in the Jewish Theological Seminary
(while I killed time on my penultimate
visit to New York, waiting)

would be more appreciative.

Like a congregation you might have had if things had worked out
    differently.

And you said you didn't mind if I went off for an hour.

All right, all right.

Remember I never said you weren't good at unforeseeable moves.

What I just said?

Never mind. But how you can know Mexico as you claim to do

(God forbid you should step foot in Israel some time. God forbid.)

without bothering to immerse yourself in Prescott's history is beyond me.

History is beyond me. And with every year you picked up fewer books.
Why is knowing the news as it happens so bloody important?

By the time I was twenty-one I was steeped in the great commentaries—
and when I got to Israel and sat at Buber's knees

no higher I hope

you can be sure I knew my history,
to say nothing about the rituals
which you couldn't be bothered to study,
much less learn, much less graze,
during the months you spent living high,
your nose in poetry (without rhyme)
and novels (without characters), made-up
worlds, when you ought to have been
gazing at bougainvillea, mountain ranges,
and ravines (chockfull with the unburied dead)
like your friend The Consul—who you'll admit had worse
jobs than I did and drank infinitely more—

—but he wasn't real—

or obsessing, letting yourself be consumed,
eaten alive by concern for a woman
who wouldn't think twice if you did disappear
forever when you left the room;
but had you taken the public bus
as your, (I must admit, well-chosen) friend D.
urged you to do, wasting his vocal register on
stubborn ears as I did until I said to hell with it, it's your
life; D. who from the years he spent at high risk in Brazil
(engaged in activities you never . . . divulged)

you who think of sneaking a box of Havana cigars
over the Canadian border as "smuggling"   w   o   w   .

How would you like to risk being frisked at customs in a country
where it's customary for people not to return from simple errands,
wearing gold charms, chains, and bracelets
up to your armpits under your shirt?

*But had you listened to D., who knew what was up
in the Third World as well as any white man his age in the real
world, you would have been spared*

the doldrums of time squandered at the Virgin of Guadeloupe's nar-
cissistic gift shop, and the guide's rote recitation (or was it a

recording?) of how the women "crawl from all over Mexico" (*we'll*
spare each other the recitation of states, ok? ok) "to pray

here,

and believe me that by the time they reach the steps where I am stand-
ing now they are exhausted,"

—*and as you reported to me with compassion (see, the "Brain" remem-*
bers) "hurting bad because each day they destroy the scabs that form
on their bloody knees at night," to which his numbness felt compelled
to reply

> "but they don't care, they're healed by prayer, they come here to
> be healed"

the stench of the church's rabid shameless exploitation of the poor,
the return in the frantic rush hour traffic, when, as the driver now
pushed the rattletrap black sedan for all it was worth,
V-8 engine whizzing past Chapultapec
Park with an   urgency   that stood the languor of the drive on its
    head—

though even that is deceptive since the increase in forward trajectory doubled the unmufflered vehicle's growl—

I still caught sight of a little boy on a tricycle being
sideswiped by a truck that pushed and weaved mercilessly . . .
as if an escaping terrorist were at the wheel, hell-bent,

and I asked the guide to stop   and when he wouldn't or seemed   not
    to hear
I opened the door to a chorus of *oh my god don't*

as if riding in an open car meant death when it means life   freedom
    air

but it might have taken you longer to ingest, to really take in, the
    Mexican
metaphor, **the unspeakably**   *tragic   incompatibility of*
Indian Mayan Aztec   Mexico   and   Christian Spanish Mexico

And the weary, prematurely gray-haired guide said: "If you do that I
will have to . . ."
And I said: "Did you see?"
"See? See what?"
"The boy . . . go under . . . and . . . no one's doing anything . . ."
"I'm sorry about the boy."

Who by now was out of sight.

At least he did not deny . . .

"I have a family too. But this is Mexico young man and you can see"
(waves his hand out the window)
"what the traffic is like. There is no way I can . . ."

"A phone then . . ."

An afternoon that would have induced a sharp
rise in the blood-pressure of an ant.

(Or praying mantis, wronged for so long.
Hey, what's the response up there

to the refutation of the accepted notion
that the female devours the male
after he has had his way with her
and she with him?

*Good. The destruction of destructive
shibboleths is always regarded as a positive sign.*

Always? I'm suspicious.)

The four women, divided, shook their heads dolefully.
Talked no more of offering the living to the dead,
the unforgiving, the superstitious, the nonexistent.
A purse-search would justify their looking down,
and God knows what those urchins might have done
when the women were occupied with cameras and beat
after the difficult climb and distracted by the sun.

"Señor, it is not our business.
And I have another . . ."

I looked back at the seething congestion.
A still unmade movie of hell.

6

*A stranger shot a Polaroid of you and Laura
side by side in the boat on your way back from Jalapa.*

I have no defense.
I didn't know someone was aiming a camera at us.
Laura took one look.
She always photographed so you could hear
a skillful slide-guitar in the background.

But you, you were variable. Moody.

"It's a good picture," Laura allowed, in her vaguely nasal whine.
"But you don't really look like that."

As if ecstasy in the crystal glitter
under an angel-riddled waterfall,
was an everyday thing.

Her radar picking up the twinge *he's feeling good,*
she shape-shifted instantaneously into a grotesque
semblance of my father, purveying
specious and gratuitous "hard truths" and "facts"
under the auspices of "reality."

—Perhaps if my experience of life had been other than it was
I might have been more sympathetic

to the ones who see you differently than you see yourself?
And say no to your unreal wishes.
For the world to be. Other than it is.

Didn't you . . . chime in . . . too?

Yeah: when I caught you after Sunday school
with that mascara-crazed vamp with the wild black hair
out of a low-budget vampire flick

like Barbara Steele in *Black Sunday*

in the dust of that faded purple curtain fronting the temple's stage
reserved for special events,
like plays the little children performed on Purim.

It wasn't she who bothered you; it was that a Jew should come from the
lower-middle class.

—*Or when I got the thrilling news that you'd been* absent
the second semester of your sophomore year at Highland High,
driving my two-toned Dodge without so much as a license
whenever possible . . . ; so yes,
I guess you could say at that time I too said no to your—
or so they sounded then—fantastical propositions.

But I also remember the happy accidents,
like the time you went to the track in Denver:
you bet on a horse named Saint
Exupery for no reason at all (god forbid
you should have consulted his record!)
except that it was the only name you recognized
and the odds were something like 50-1 against him
and he won—

placed—

won

Either way you came out ahead on the day.

Chance was the real victor.

It depends what you mean by chance.

7

(Laura)

I'm portraying her as crueler than she was.
I don't think she was this way
with anyone, randomly.

Like her upstairs neighbor, the pipe-smoking mystery writer,
who of course wanted to fuck her but rested content.
(She said you two would like each other and she was right.)

It was as if out of sheer perversity I had switched off
my high beams at night on a remote country road
where WARNING signs were clearly posted: **DEER
CROSSING**, or **BEWARE SHARP TURNS**, or
BRIDGE FREEZES BEFORE ROAD SURFACE.

By ignoring these warnings I set myself up to take the fall.

Many reasons remain obscure but the one that later stood out
like a burning brand hurled into the icy night,
was that her cruelty was a way of getting me to back off, of
letting me know that my ardor was wasted on her,
and that the sooner I abandoned pursuit of a woman who *was not
    there,*
the better off, happier, freer,

and—alone again—I'd be—

❧

Back to life alone—to women I liked to make love to,
and wished would vanish the instant after;
women I liked to look at;
women I liked to hang with.

Never the combination in one woman.

And why couldn't there be a reversal as in so many
novels, plays, and 30's movies?

Why? It's your call.

8

(Like Teens in an Asylum Movie)

No one could have warned anyone more
or made more clear what couldn't happen
in the traumatic aftermath of the rape
in the stairwell of her walk-up.

With more shrinks than trees in The Naked City
she chose to train each week to Philly
to see Willem. And demanded I
accompany her or "end it now."

I thought we'd entered the wrong office.
The waiting room overflowed with other
young long-haired types who lived in denim.
All the women abjured bras; (several were

breast-feeding). Welcome to the domain
of Dr. Willem Keen. A small fleshy dude
who wore a lime-colored tee shirt
and brown, baggy gabardines.

Which was the source of some shock
since the classic psychoanalyst is born
wearing muted suits and ties, mysterious
weaves of gray and brown.

And yet it didn't take forever
to figure out that the absence of air-
conditioning was a choice, as was
the light-cotton shift Laura had worn.

There was a sofa and may have been a chair
but I remember the scatter of cushions—
the delectable option of being horizontal.
Like a lot of people who affect a casual

air, he went straight to the point.
"The rape brought out earlier traumas which I
have begun, after many detours, to unearth."
Skip the archaeological metaphors, I thought.

"You know about her father. And how he took
giving his daughter baths a little too far."
"But Laura said she'd worked through . . ."
"She was almost there. The rape

was an immeasurable setback.
For now. And for the next few years
she's an emotional vegetable."
"How can you say that . . . as if she weren't human."

I gave my spiel about how I was willing to wait for her to recover.
"She's frozen."
I gave him my best highly skeptical look.
"There's no reason why you should understand."

Laura squeezed my hand. Whispered in my ear.
Sultry voiced in the sultriness. That she "liked me."
Then (more audibly): "*Please. Listen* to Willem."
This was a doc you called by his first name.

"But I like Laura."
"I like her too. But there is no Laura."
Our arms around each other now as we huddled close,
like teens in an asylum movie.

"You're looking for intimacy . . . don't be ashamed!
Get it from another woman."
How could he have guessed so fast that I was mortally
tired of inaptly named "relationships" built around sex,

and that I was in the grip of something I found
bizarrely alluring in the case of Laura . . . ?
Laura; like melted wax.
Her dress rolled-up now to hip level.

"Once we defuse these . . . bombs in her system
she *may* come back to life, burst free of the pod . . . ,
but it will take . . . years."
He sensed I was bursting to interrupt:

"I'm giving it to you straight."
Reclining in the moist oppressive heat
she and I found murderous
he gave a charge to every word.

"The woman you see hear smell and touch . . .
Her skin is warm and smooth,
her copper hair is luminous in the summer sun,
her cunt is wet—and that's the most deceptive—

because inside, inside her insides
she feels nothing; she's . . ."
(reaches across the room to squeeze her wrist)

"NUMB"

"But if she's frigid how come she's so open.
There was a girl in Colorado.
She lay on her back with her thighs shut
and a terrified expression."

"And you let go.
You didn't force the issue."
"Maybe I felt more friendly than amorous
and that look, combined with the way

she pressed her thighs together
while lying there naked
on the rug in that sanguine
light, made persistence seem absurd."

"But you were angry." "No, frustrated.
I also had the misfortune of knowing her father
(who gloated when he whipped me at tennis
after I told him I never played) and figured

her misery was rooted in his shitheadedness.
And we'd both be gone from town before the end of summer."
"But nothing Laura or I say can make you see
that this situation is the same in a different form."

"No, in the other case a more gentle and patient . . .
approach . . . might have been the key . . .
it pains me to say . . . and I want Laura."
"There is that difference.

They're pounding on my door—session's over.
I think we—I mean the three of us—should meet again."
And he was gone. And she and I were never closer
than in the silence we dwelled in on the ride home.

26

9

Voice Mask

Was there something in the lay of your arrangement
that kept an edge honed that so often grows flat-dull
in the "relationships" characterized as normal;
those in which the couples accommodate, "learn to live"
with each other—and the flaws that make them more human?

No.

But whenever she consented, whenever
she jettisoned, suspended, waylaid,
the latent condition which the rape had forced

to its somatic source,

she was ready; she was as—
accommodating—as any woman who looked

forward to sex (and, however decorous
and unforthcoming, having shed their layers, verging
on apparatus: the sweaters, skirts, shoes, bras, panty-hose, and socks),
leaving panties on—for one reason, another, and another—
as they crawled quickly between the sheets,
so as to encourage further conversation

that led us toward this quiet

intimacy, as if no boy/man could withstand plunging in, if—

—No, following her ablutions Laura simply
got into her bed, and on those

rare occasions when she wanted

company, issued a summons like
"you can come in with me if you want to"

in a girlish slash angelic twang.

The first few times she grew so wet and wide
I thought we'd moved to another plane.
The body doesn't lie. Not there. Not in
that way. I couldn't read her face when my
eyes and lips and tongue lifted
from their delectable explore, while I
moved, or was taken further and further in.
Then, in the semi-meek timbres our ambivalence adopts
when we don't want to incur the unpredictable wrath of
someone whom we're about to disappoint,
none more lethal than lovers,
who can't turn back—
not now—she'd ask if I could come.
In the gushing forth, I gasped; and in
oblivion's knell swallowed: deception.

Center split. Treble division.

10

(Damning the Messenger)

How did you meet Laura?

In my apartment.

That doesn't seem real.

She had stopped to pick up a mutual
friend—and I conspired to have *her* stay.

She groaned how she was starving,
    and touched   her stomach—

(hard to conceive then that someone so thin
could obsess so ferociously about food).

My one room flat quickened intimacies.

I took the desk chair, Jenny the sofa, and Laura,
as if to complete a triangle, perched on the edge of
the only item I had not found on the street.
(Which thank God I had had the foresight to
throw a bedspread over before this stranger arrived!)

"If you're starving I know a place on MacDougal."

Laura was a good hour late for a "prior engagement" and soon
Jenny would have to catch the "seven-something"
back to her parents' house—(don't ask me why the hurry
unless she . . . sensed?)—where she was holed-up
while she pounded the unpromising, promiscuous streets
searching for work.

"But I'm sure you two will have . . . a *wonderful* dinner . . .
and I'll see you . . . and *you* . . . soon . . ."

❧

We had to pass my apartment to get to Laura's—which was further
    west.

She might as well come up given the way the evening had—

Once full, she groaned of gone hungers, and no
sooner reassumed her position on the bed than I proposed
she spend the summer with me in Cuernavaca

(where the plan to share a villa with some college friends
in the social sciences who'd planned to
study at The Institute with The Master—
including D. and a married couple—
had just fallen through).

She didn't say a single expected thing.
No "we only just met it's absurd" stuff;
every disclaimer revolved around her "full-time job"
from which "there was no way" she could take an unpaid leave.

My willingness to survive as an office temp
provoked her contempt.

"How can you, who don't have a real job, understand?"

This in the tone of Hannah Arendt to students who wanted shortcuts:
"How can you, who haven't read [Schopenhauer], understand
what [Nietzsche] is getting at?"

Once it was clear the rent was taken care of

(I had salted away the money for the Mexican venture)

the idea began to interest her—

we had a roller-coaster week, warnings, provisos
desires, complicities, misgivings.

You must have come to an agreement.

That's what it was.

So no problem?

One. I believed the terms would change.

That you would prove an exception.

That she didn't say the things she said.

I couldn't prepare myself for the unexpected hurts.

How she couldn't forgive me my friendship
with someone she found as unglamorous as Jenny.

Through whom you met?

I guess you could say that.

Why do we all imagine, when it comes to character,
that what has befallen others will not necessarily befall us?

That we will be spared.

What made you think of Laura now?

I was as surprised as you are.

11

Where She Could Be Found

I was on my way to meet someone a few blocks
south of the area I used to haunt
in Greenwich Village, took the IRT a stop past

Christopher to Varick and there it loomed,
like an ancient amphitheater, but not in ruins—
the hangout she so often alluded to. I

never went. My aversion was complete:
even after she and I were long
finished, and I had gone back to live

in a neighborhood I loved, I never
once caught sight of the sign **CARMINE STREET POOL**
that blazed out with a faded grandeur.

Now I saw her slouching in with the catch-all straw bag
she had earlier purchased in Mexico slung over her shoulder,
lying there on a towel in all her tawny allure

to be ogled by "older men" (approaching forty)
whom she "liked to go with because their sexual demands were less,"
and male models who "weren't gay";

her element—though she never mentioned swimming—:
only men, men who would not impinge or demand or inflict . . .
so she could keep the necessary distance.

On the few nights in Mexico either she had come
or I was delusional, she had an answer
over omelets, "yes . . . , I was turned on

by the [male] lead in [such and such] movie . . .";
and the night after we were let go
after our abduction by the cops and near

incarceration in a Mexican
jail, she became—like a spirit set free.
Maybe danger was her true element.

Where the Story Leaves Off

We had set out, the four of us, like pilgrims.
It's a quick jaunt to Guanajuato from San Miguel,
over long stretches of restless earth,
not desert, not valley,
patchy green on tawny ground,
head to head in the passing lane
with a pick-up sprouting children
and a blunderbuss fifties' Chevy
with no hood over its engine, with its insides exposed.
A quick jaunt to the underworld, the gauzy mummies.
But we lingered in the marketplace:
the two women—my cousin's wife, my lover—
poring over shawls and serapes;
my cousin clicking away with his Nikon and zoom
at the gargoyles' leering and capricious faces,

while I lost myself among the hawkers' masks—
swinging like lanterns on the standards—
blessed and damned with edgy, angular,
yet impassive facades.
And made of no special wood.
I wanted one anyway and forked out eight pesos.
It's hard crawling through the crypt.
You have to get down on your hands and knees
and the openings were meant
for smaller people, unless the getting down
was part of a solemn ritual.
It was a relief to be in the cool of the underworld,
away from the tension of the light.
The dead were well preserved.
They stood upright. They stayed together.

I couldn't have known it then, but soon
my cousin, his wife, my lover—soon
we would all be lost to each other forever—
not taken by death,

just gone into another kind of dust.

THE GUITAR LESSON

1

But your analysis as to why he behaved this way may also be off the wall, or belong to the fringe of reason and reality, because your mother treated you with a similar exasperation, with an entirely different, if not opposite, set of circumstantial details with regard to where you lived and whom you lived with. She tried everything and nothing took.

From her point of view.

But you were resistant.

Or disaffected.

She did schlep you to guitar lessons in one of those small towns south of Chicago. And later paid for a piano teacher to come to your apartment in Salt Lake City. And nothing took.

No, everyone was too gung ho, like they were selling a product.

Which in essence

they *weren't.* All they had to sell was time. I was easing into the guitar, I was easing into working out my assignment on an el cheapo acoustic, limp nylon strings, light as varnished balsawood, but it pained my senses to play "Old McDonald Had a Farm," even when I could do it with marginal fluency.

In other words, if he'd given you the chords to "Hound Dog" . . . and held out another song you loved as bait . . .

like "Runaway," I might have persisted.

But what's wrong with starting from scratch.

Where's scratch? I was somewhere near the nebulous ineffable "scratch" when I was dropped at the door of their small two story house, white on the outside, lawn clipped so close it could have passed for artificial turf, and . . .

What's the matter?

From the overgrown violet shag rug, like a lawn that could have used some cutting, to the vicious green sofa, the brightness of the primary colors inside the house made me dizzy. "You relax, they'll be here any moment. My boys know better than to be late."

The room was so silent and devoid of any sign of life I wanted to ask where they were, but I never had the chance. The four sons appeared, converged rather, at the same instant from different parts of the house. One emerged from an adjacent door I assumed was a closet. Another said "hi there" while he clambered jauntily down the stairs. Another rose from the cellar, another descended from the attic. I stifled a laugh when I imagined another brother exiting from the fireplace . . .

Each wore a dazzlingly busy and colorful western shirt with glaring, light-reflecting metal snap buttons. Within moments they had plugged their electric guitars into gargantuan speakers I had only seen on display at music stores. They launched into a jam session. At first I was fascinated. But after fifteen minutes they showed no sign of stopping. I became restless, uncomfortable. And I wasn't alone: the sounds blasted at such a high decibel pitch that the ashtrays, mirrors, and china began to shake. Terrified windows rattled, and clutched the panes to steady themselves. I didn't know how to get their attention except by screaming and there was more than one obvious reason not to offend this decent, clean-cut, well intentioned family. They might have read my thoughts, or sensed something in my expression, because they stopped as abruptly as they started. The father asked me what I thought. "Amazing," was the best I could do. "You can get there. Don't you think so boys?" "Sure, once you don't have to look at what your fingers are doing you can do anything. Have you ever played an electric?" "No." "Try mine." After a few strums I was invited to "play that song you've been rehearsing" on whatever electric guitar I liked best. "I'm a little tired of Old McDonald." "That's all right, once you can play it perfect we'll find you a song you'll like." I was veritably heartsick, nauseous, and never, *never*, reentered the house.

How could you take something like that so hard?

I have no words for how I felt, nausea and dread made the decision for me. I never went back.

There must have been other guitar teachers, even in a town that small.

Even if there were, I withdrew, and contented myself with improvising alone in my room.

Which didn't bring the satisfaction of mastery.

There were other satisfactions. And what have you got against bongo drums and tambourines and the sounds you can extract from glass and wood with objects ranging from utensils to pens. When everyone in my sixth grade class was asked to do some kind of performance alone, I chose to play the piano.

I don't remember any mention of piano lessons at this juncture.

Purpose dignifies . . .

2

"Performance Day," Sixth Grade

I decided to plan nothing in advance.
Thought of the instrument as a living organism.
Perched on the bench.
Drummed on the wood with the flat palm bongo method.
Struck a few black keys sharply.
Managed a few somber chords:
held until the hum subsided.
Banged out dissonances gently with my fists
my elbows and my forehead,
climbed on, made a racket,
then saw myself tapping empty glasses and utensils
killing time in restaurants,

hopped off, asked if someone
could throw me a pen.

Tapped the instrument now there now here
with long pauses in between
as if testing reflexes,
my body becoming one
with this disused, dusty, and neglected object,
and its strange and unfamiliar
sounds that could have gone
unheard, in the custody of music teachers,
hired by the county,
who once a week for an hour
moved from scales to pre-Muzak standards
with the excruciating slowness of the speech
people use to make themselves
understood by the deaf.

3

Once I sensed the class was liking it and not laughing *at* me I lost
myself in the rapturous dissonance.

So when you first heard, say, Rite of Spring, *your response was: I recog-
nize that.*

It's not like you to leap ahead a decade, but yes, when I first heard
Stravinsky, Schoenberg, and Berg—who intrigued me in ways I
wouldn't have dared attempt to articulate—I sighed with immense,
even immeasurable relief. A light bulb with a (?) inside it appeared
over my head as in a cartoon.

What was the question?

That's a good question.

I never thought of answering.

I wondered why no one had ever said
suggested hinted or insinuated
that there was another way,
a way to make an art
out of wrong notes.

Wait. I have left out one piece of crucial information. I never would have had the nerve to risk making an ass of myself if I didn't know, deep down, that my teacher loved me that year.

Loved?

Don't hang on my words that way. Since we know that two out of my last three elementary school teachers loathed me, and probably would have ejected me if they had had the technology, I mean the legal grounds, the opportunity, I permit myself the use of the word "love" in a sense that is appropriate between a ten-year-old boy and a thirtyish female teacher who, far from being a spinster-type, had lovely long dark hair with thick curls, and the right figure for the zebra patterned sweaters and tight skirts she favored.

She was hot.

I liked her too much to look at her in a more detached, purely sexual way. On the final day of elementary school she told the class she wouldn't be Miss Daltry much longer.

To your consternation. Confusion. Disbelief.

I don't know why I found it so hard to believe. She said her fiancé was the manager of the local Thom McCann. My parents said he was a very nice man.

They knew him even though your mother would never stoop to purchase shoes there?

I think he was a member of Rotary. And in a small town the people who work in shops on Main Street are highly visible.

You could have been happy for her . . .

It was the shock. I knew I'd miss her. The announcement just made it utterly clear that she wasn't going to be a factor in my life after sixth grade.

She was and is.

Let's say . . . she liked about me the very qualities that the others loathed . . . and fostered my best behavior . . . and performance in class . . . so that by the end of the year I sat right behind the smartest, classiest girl in the class . . . to whom I was almost proud to lose the spelling bee.

Yeah right.

No, she was exemplary; a class act; no mixed signals.

Describe.

Extraordinarily tall. Brown hair, worn long, braided. Father some kind of—high-powered lawyer.

A man with more than a single way of viewing the world.

She was—advanced—way more—developed

physically . . .

spiritually, intellectually, than the rest of us. Could have passed for a teenager. Why do you steer our dialogues toward the painful, the humiliating, or the salacious?

Perversity.

So you're aware—

You never said what she did the day you discovered performance art?

She played something on the viola.

Figures.

And one palooka asked "what's a viola," and before she could answer some creep chimed in "it's like a violin but doesn't sound as good."

I'll bet that got her.

I don't think she heard a word.

Too tall?

Exactly.

4

"Cheif"

By fifth grade I could spell almost any word by visualizing the letters— by which I don't mean to imply I knew what all these words meant. I specialized in polysyllabic words that elementary school children rarely had the chance to use in everyday life, words like *sacrifice, abandoned* and *conspiracy.*

We stood with folded arms leaning against the radiator—our waists level with the windows. There were only two of us left in the spelling bee, the stunning Jeanne who sat in the first seat in the front row because she had the highest grades, and myself. As the teacher hurled longer and longer words across the classroom she and I were really making contact. She had long chestnut brown hair and long eyelashes and she held herself very erect. I always aimed at her when we played dodge ball at recess and she often spiritedly tried to hit me back, but we'd never had a real conversation (much less a moment alone together) since I'd moved into town earlier in the fall. She was tall, taller than me, and I felt a kind of electric charge and a longing for the contest to go on and on so we could stand side by side, our hips grazing each other. She favored knee-length pleated skirts with enough fabric for two purely functional skirts. She dressed swell, but she didn't act swell. I couldn't tell what she was feeling about winning or losing (her confidence in herself seemed boundless so how could I measure?) but I knew we were both sharing an intense erotic pleasure at our facility and ease, our sudden power, as the rest of the students, on their own accord, watched and maintained a silence worthy of a church service as the tension built. She, like me, couldn't have known the meaning of *every* word she spelled, like *anachronism* or *existentialist or sesquipedalian,* but the quickness of our responses, answering before daring to think, prompted bursts of laughter. They came in torrents, words like *witness* and *significant, Chrysler* and *apartment, joist, armature, creation. Gorgeous. Massacre. Lassitude. Courageous. Intermittent. Hennessey. Brassiere.* (I couldn't believe our teacher, a crewcut ex-forward for "the fighting Illini" threw that one in!) Double-"ess" words crept in, made me nervous. I didn't want to have to spell *successful* and *accused* will always look wrong no matter how I spell it. The origin of my demise is that the double esses made my eyes cross and I began to panic over my failure to see them in my head while Jeanne was nonplussed and fielded these knuckle-balls without missing a beat.

By now we were seated next to each other on the radiator. We hadn't heard the bell ring to mark the end of the period. We weren't aware that the other children were looking at us except to note that we were in another realm, magically free from harm and boredom. I don't know how I felt about winning or losing; I do know I didn't want anything to destroy the warmth and respect I sensed was mutual. And then the teacher—(who had told my mother he didn't like the way I looked at him)—said "chief." I tried to suppress the anxiety wildfiring in the pit of my stomach and to buy time pretended to be insulted by repeating the word in a loud voice *as if to say come on, give me something more challenging, any idiot can spell chief.* That was a bust: his hands were planted on his hips, his smile grew wider. Knowing I was done for anyway, I played the mental game I always played when asked a question that seemed so easy there had to be a trick, in this case the simple and convenient rule: "i before e except after c."

It was not *I* who then superimposed this notion, in my lightheaded blankness and vacancy, and *against every instinct crying out inside me* said "c-h-e-i-f." The teacher turned his gaze toward Jeanne, who spelled the word firmly, but softly, as if she too thought it was a pity that all the fun we were having was doomed to end on such a pitiful note. Losing to my delightful classmate was the least of my concerns (no one could take away from me the pleasure I had had in sharing that time with her) but I loathed myself for having self-destructed in this way, by panicking, by separating myself from myself. And instead of running out the door with the others when our jailer announced a special ten minute break since the spelling bee had gone on a lot longer than he had expected, I had to wait until everyone was gone from the room to look out the window and take in the bleak November day in the town where I was once again a stranger. It hadn't been so bad when we were perched together on the radiator with our backs to the grayness. What remained? Empty houses shrouded behind elms and the cold wind lashing the branches without a sound behind mean white picket fences. And I thought it odd that no one ever thought to ask if Keep Out was one word or two.

THE SHALLOWNESS OF THE LAKE

1

I couldn't resist hiking into town after I woke
until, tiring, I happened on

a universal mall and a man
wearing a sky-blue *Sweet's Candy* logo,

"It's run by Jewish people."
The Sweet son was a year younger, or older,

or went to private school, St. Marks . . . —
which may explain why I only set eyes
on him that first week in Salt Lake,

when I was living, gloriously, out of a suitcase.

How could you have forgotten that the Sweets
were in the candy business?

I never trust the first answer that comes to mind.

They were members of the congregation.
In your mother's imagination Mrs. S was her best friend.

I'm grateful for their employee's interruptions.

"There's been a lot of death in the family."

(—I had heard from my mother her friend Corinne
had passed recently into a world of light.)

"What kind of work do you do for them?"

"Delivery. I don't look like a man
who's up to his elbows in molasses, do I?"

44

His lunch-companion hee-haws, bleats, guffaws
before the sudden, violent,
stereotypical retreat into silence.

A silence of aluminum and chrome.

Oppressive reflections.

"The boy isn't in the candy business.
He's got an antique shop around the corner."

I don't understand collectors.

I dream so much of living
without a past in a hotel
it becomes my reality.

Talking to yourself again? Are you good company for you?

I'm afraid if I laugh out loud to myself,
or cry, people will think

what they want to think.
Be who you are.
Do what you have to do.
Forget the mind's midges.
Stay with the real.

What you care about.

The rest fades away, like autumn,
on the blowing of a horn.

Don't give me that "huh" look,
take another look at Jeremiah.

I could use someone like that
to help get me through this
period in my life.

Everyone could. Be grateful you're living it.

If I were still practicing I'd treat you for nothing.
Oh I know you think that psychiatrists,
(who sure know how to rake in the dough),
are better equipped to help people
than men of the cloth, but I can
assure you, I helped many and could have helped you
if you'd let me.

Why is it all right for women to have emotional outbursts in public and not for men?

❧

The mall's immensity under the sheer rubric of   FOOD

TCBY   EDO   SBARRO   SCHLOTZSKY'S

as American as the vacancy that has become
America

everything everywhere the same

cruel raid on the food chain

(" . . . daring, resourceful, like the masked rider of the plain . . .")

It's your generation made it that way, son.

Someone must have sown the seeds, no?

You are stubborn. Can't remember if I had a hand in that or
if you were that way when I became your father.

(Silence.)

Freud said character is fixed at six.

You've no . . . rejoinder to that one?

46

(Silence.)

Nothing?

Is there anything you like?

The nearness of gardens.

The nearness of mountains.

The nearness of god?

—I find his absence more reassuring.

The high Victorian houses in the heights.

—Let me once again look down from the mountain
heights into this basin, glittering
like a bracelet or the night
itself, open to anyone.

The Peery (Hotel)

Desperate for tea and honey. I don't mind supplying the tea. Why can't
hotels across the world supply customers with hot water?

You wouldn't have been in such a passion for tea and honey
if that dentist hadn't drilled your tongue right before
your plane lifted off into the night
for Salt Lake . . . where . . . —I see I'd better refresh
your memory—altitude
is a factor, the blood
wells, rushes to the fore;
nosebleeds are commonplace.

Something like that happened in Durango:
my lips cracked and bled in no time at all.

No one warned me that this always happens
in the dryness of the high chaparral.

Why does everyone underplay . . .

The dangers of living.

When they could just
                    not look down.

And on ski-slopes Easterners would kill to go down you

had the distinct sense that the mountain was concave
and that if I went down I'd hurtle off into whiteness:
one graceless frantic somersault.

2

We made the rounds after we arrived in Salt Lake.
The Silver family ran their home movies.

The Silver Family Skiers

waving to the camera with an implicit
*this is what you can look forward to
in Utah, lucky   you*

which display had the identical effect on me
as the guitar concert in Kankakee.

                                    "I'll pass."

My mother fumed.
"They give you free introductory skiing
lessons . . . and I . . . just don't understand

why you don't take advantage . . .
I just don't get it . . . why you don't . . ."

Heights? Whiteness?
Cold?

The Silvers lived on skis.

None of the kids I met in Junior High skied. Why? Because skiing,
   after the
Free Introductory Lesson,
was hardly free; it was beyond their families' reach;

*and if they earned money after school the church took ten percent off the
top.*

*We're talking 1965. Boom time. (Kennedy had been blasted but the coun-
try could do nothing wrong where $ was concerned . . .) Thirty years have
passed and today* USA TODAY *featured this item on the front page: "Top
ski lift tickets schuss past $50 . . . higher fees may be discouraging begin-
ners." History could catch up with you.*

We lived just south of the line that runs across the valley, 7th East,
which divided rich and poor in Salt Lake City.

By the time I got to Highland High the kids came to school on skis.

I was born yesterday, right.

Well, in ski-sweaters (tight weave, one stripe), ski-boots.

And hats, don't let me forget the hats, with those pompoms.

As if dressed for a night's wholesome yodeling.

Social class defined itself by who
hit the slopes on the weekend.

(And were often next seen again wearing plaster casts.)

And who hit the public golf courses before daybreak
to get in a free nine holes before forking over the albeit fair
75¢ greens fee for a second nine. All went well until

Joseph Smith, the blonde, brawny, adolescent-loathing
assistant-pro crept up behind us as we teed off on the fourth—
a water hole that was all carry, all hundred yards.

(How I loved the challenge—edge to edge.
The hole—placed by the devil himself.
Go for the flag, risk the ball backing up into the water.
Go for the fat of the green, risk the woods behind.)

"I think you guys are somewhere you shouldn't be."

I didn't even think about trying to talk myself out of this one.

"I'm tempted to wrap those clubs around your neck."

Dark the lake, murky.
Creature friendly; too small for monsters.

"But we're in birdie range!"

"LISTEN KID I'M GOING EASY ON YOU . . ."

I knew when to back down, assume
mildly contrite downcast expression
to show you're ashamed at what you've done.

That's the charade.

—I wasn't much for lessons.

❧

The Silvers represented the good life.

And decency too yes decency.

Like a TV family.

I didn't say it.

Come winter, they disappeared
onto the slopes—.

I once went down
Alta in a toboggan.
Whirled. Rolled.
Spun. Toppled.

That was more like it:
grounded free-fall.
Snow crept and slithered
through every aperture.

I wanted to know how wet
and cold I could get
without, you know, the worst
happening.

❧

Gangrene was such a movie moment
I burst out laughing when my mother
told me how they chopped off
her best friend's husband's leg . . .

This is the kindness you return
the rough-hewn, gruff yet benign,
tie salesman who, hirsute
in a sleeveless undershirt,
wheeled the two-year-old you
along the Hudson beside his infant son
on muggy Sundays in Manhattan?

Facts I know from photographs.

So you don't actually remember.

Only the way he later always
pinched my cheek and said, "Hiya kid."

Nothing more before later?

No, but the faded images stir . . .

Recognition?

There are as many ways to die
as there are people.

Gangrene isn't something you get hanging out
on East 57th Street; it's the property of the Scotts, or the
    Amundsens . . . ,

and their dogs

or characters in modernist novels who wander into snowy   wastes.
—Or the moment after the shoot-out when they inspect your leg
while you're still on your horse and
hiss with sympathy as the decision is made whether to cut it off
(—your leg—with whiskey as the sole anesthetic—)
or let you die. Or shoot you dead. If you ask nicely enough.
Gangrene second only to the quicksand scene you could sense was
    coming,
when a bumpkin infantryman would wade in—
holding his bayonet-equipped M-1 high—
to test the depths, and find his weapons and helmet
useless. The platoon
useless
when it came to rescuing him . . . —for in this jungle clearing there is
    not one
branch long enough or strong enough to give the men a chance to
    yank him out
of the drink.

(They'd have been better off in a western,
tying a rope to a horse's pommel.)

Or they never arrive, remain waiting to hear
whether or not he encountered enemy fire.

Either way, a final gurgle before the cut to a stunned platoon.

Before the captain, exchanging cigar stub for pencil stub,
writes a letter to his mom and pop on another private's back.

3

Indecency

The East was already . . . in the tapered look

like The Fugs.

with eyes peeled toward the mini-skirt . . .
So by the time I was "seven . . . tee . . . n . . ."
and Sinatra's lugubrious refrain
droned from every car and bar
in the wake of Dino's "Houston"

like a 45 played on 33

I wanted to yell   "spit it out!"

You were *seventeen. Impatient too . . .*

Whose idea do you think it was to see The Fugs?
So that when Barbara and I sat in the front row at Fillmore
East, one of those ragged heroes could leap,
mike-in-hand, from the stage and crawl right under her . . . skirt—
his unwashed mane tickling her thighs with a pirate's flair as I . . .
underwent d-d dis-comfort,

even shame at my lack . . . of cool . . .
becoming invisible, the disguise I then
found acceptable however awful it felt,
and I, who never stuttered, stuttered with rage.

She eluded you and you eluded yourself. And she was precocious, like your cousin in LA who at fifteen was dating the lead singer of a hot group with an animal name

Animals. Byrds. Turtles. (Anything but the prefabricated Monkees.)

and you were   anything but.

OK.

Do you think those years in Salt Lake City left me unmarked?

Mark unmarked, I'd like to roll that one on my tongue. I wonder if my colleagues in the afterlife would go for that or if it's too private.

If it's just a matter of information, what better have you got to do to
  occupy your time

exiled from *Jim Beam* and *Old Taylor*

and what about the sour mash, the Jack Daniel's, Maker's Mark, *and* Rebel Yell *I laid in for your visits.*

Visits! More in-frequent they couldn't have been.

Bourbon's better than sour mash. You just thought the sour mash was better because it was more expensive . . . and in the air, as Absolut *is now and* P. F. Flyers *were when you were little and believed they helped you run faster, just as you begged me to buy TV's and cars on layaway plans—only $29.99 a month and you could buy*

the world.

I wasn't going to say it.

I never thought it through. But it did tickle me to engage you in these high-spirited arguments about meaningless things. You enjoyed repeating how you "laid-in the expensive stuff" for your "son's" visit. And I enjoyed asking innocent questions, such as why you kept looking at your watch as the hands approached five-in-the-afternoon.

And you'd mutter something about when the next "important news
program" would come on the air.

Why do you think it is so painful to go back to Salt Lake?

And then at 37,000 ft instead of a mere 37 stories in the dentist's chair,
the woman riding beside you in the night asks if she should try

scuba-diving in the Great
Salt Lake.

I like that "great."

So do the salt companies.

Robert Smithson pointed
to what the salt crystal's spiral
might reveal about the real.

Did I ever step foot in the lake?
Or would I now answer
on the distantly recalled
testimony of my schoolmates,
none of whom, if I remember
rightly, ever did more than that—
they did not swim, did not
step in, go under,
just let their bodies taste
the buoyancy

the lake is famous for

I opened my eyes after a minute's meditation
and saw a few sailboats within
the mountain bowl,
desolate, yet desultory mariners,
dreaming of waters teeming

with creatures of the deep,
        fish!—
and not the one sign of life in these waters—
brine-shrimp, muddy, moody,
unfit for human consumption or use as bait.
Only gulls go for them.

These crustaceans lift their eyes to the light

glitter of gull's eyes

for an instant before the sinister wing-shadow
envelops them, and the strong, flexible, adaptable beak
traps the pathetic bottom-dwellers.

Forget the city. It would help if you named this section The Shallowness
of the Lake.

And then, to my amazement,

*you should be used to the dice turning up this way by now, allow me if I
cut to the fact that*

the same three triangular white sails
were all I could see on the expanse of
"water" when the return

flight passed over

on as conspicuously clear an autumn morning
as the country of God's chosen can
offer

gulls wheeling in emptiness
less than vast
over dry plateau
less than desert
over foothills
less than green

That was kind of you to share your Walkman earphones with the woman
in the next seat who had never heard Iris Dement sing in her Missouri
twang, "An arm's just an arm till it's wrapped round a shoulder . . ."

It was just a ruse. A way
of being, if not   face to face,
at least   cheek to cheek.

How do you know?

One of the last things we talked about,
at my insistence, was the quality of
eros on the home front.

I see them as conjoint operations.
Both insist I submit
to my nature.

Well you were affectionate.

You too.

All right then. I won't press
you on this one.

The desk clerk at the Peery lavished you with spring water at her
employee's discount and lent you magazines you had no reason to buy.
Why?

It was from her favorite spring, drinks it all the time, and "why should
you pay $4.00 for something you're going to look at and throw away?
Just bring them back when you check out."

Tell me the name of that hotel again? That's half of half of what it would
go for at the mini-bar.

No mini-bar.

That's ok. What time do the State Liquor Stores close now?

From Saturday evening to the day after Columbus Day.

What time. I asked for the time . . .

I can't do better than evening.

Between 5 and 8?

And since desk clerks notoriously soak you for every shekel they can

(How to Succeed in Business By Really Trying)

you asked how long she'd worked there and she answered
"two weeks, just since I got out of prison."

"What for?"

(You, in prison, when with your firm frame fair hair and modicum of freckles you look like Pippi Longstocking "fifteen years later . . ." Or her precursor and double who came back from unearthing the first dinosaur bone on this continent with her braids turned up, tips aflame, like exclamation points in Spanish!)

"Driving drunk while still on probation."

"For what?"

"Credit card fraud. I was in jail a year . . ."

You'd hardly know it.

As if there were some stigmata that clung; some visible sign . . . When will you learn that life is not a walk across a field.

Getting to like her more and more.

Whoever strives upwards.

What would Guy de Maupassant have guessed about her past on one of his instructional outings with uncle Gustave?

Before or after she started offering discounts?

Maybe . . . it comes down to . . . people . . . like animals . . .

—*who are animals may I remind you*—

recognize each other . . .

and still do on account of your . . . interruptions . . .

How's your tongue?

Don't ask. I'm sticking on words . . .

It's true I visited you to keep your soul from withering as Kol Nidre
    approached
in the thick, sickening air of your unlivable city;
                                     but then you
opened the door when I knocked

once. I had to turn to god
to be up-
lifted, taken
out of my soul's darkening nights

and while I wagered, like your
austere Jansenist friend,

that was later—before he became "serious"
he spent more time at the gaming tables than at prayer . . .

                    your "Blaze"
Pascal, that the guy up there was listening
and did his goddamnest

to give me the courage
to face indifferent congregations

or rebuffs from my wife.

Sometimes it's not enough
to ponder Job's plaguesores
when you're suffering in a thoroughly modern way.

A man can't live on god alone.

But he could have done something,
no?, to keep that Seattle Mariner Martinez
from smashing a goddamn grand slam—

Wouldn't your beloved Greeks concur
that seven RBI's in one game is
too much for any one man.

Any *man.*

(That hitter's bat was silent in his next
twenty-something times at the plate.
Why is life always like that?)

Only He can answer that.
Only He can answer that.

But you can't expect a rejected deity
to be summoned by your doubt-riddled
skeptical crew.

Spirits don't log onto the Internet,
and the answer to your ingenuous
question never stops blazing in his Book,
whether or not anyone opens it.

Another—age of heroes . . .

Cancel nothing out. And try to be more observant. See if you can see
what those two canny observers might have derived from the desk
clerk's behavior.

PERSEUS AND ANDROMEDA

I. PERSEUS SURPRISED, ANDROMEDA UNBOUND

The gods have not created men.
Men have created the gods.
— HOLDERLIN

1

How Perseus Caught Himself Before He Fell

In order that this story occur and another flight
not be delayed by weather's chaos,
Aeolus ordered the wind to give way to stillness
at dawn. The morning star pried open
Perseus' eyes, and in the grip of this magnetic
radiance he leapt

out of bed, grabbed
his saber, clamped wings to sandals,
and was soon at cruising altitude.
He found nothing more intoxicating
than to be up where the air was clear.
Horizonless distances: pure possibility.

He passed over Nubia and the Nile.
Remembered the headlines:
TROUBLED GOVERNMENTS.
A cliff drew near.
A relief came into view:
a female form; bare

but for a woven
silver band around her neck;
a stone woman—hands and feet
chained to a rockface where wind
lashed her hair across her face.
He hovered like a hummingbird.

If he'd known it was rude to stare
he would not have seen her eyes fill
with warm tears and, as the jutting frieze
unfroze, he was seized: stricken.
High-minded, fearless, yet fragile,
and very young, he was utterly

at the mercy of having seen
a woman as a woman for the first time.
That she was gorgeous beyond belief
tore Perseus out of his body: the half-god
courted free fall, almost forgetting
that to stay aloft he had to beat his wings.

Recognizing his life's love
the instant he saw her come alive
he resolved to win her hand.
Appalled to see one so innocent
chained down for her mother Cassiopeia's
inexcusable gaffe instead of

being bound—to him—in love
and marriage, he barraged her
with questions: "Where are you from?
What is the reason that they use you thus?
Who tied you to this rockface
in these desolate heights?"

He was so much inside his own story
he noted only her physical bind
and was blind to what another hero
more experienced in stuff like love
at first sight might have asked himself:
"Does she love me too?"

Since Andromeda was taking the fall
for her narcissistic mother's absence
of impulse control in telling Neptune
that her beauty exceeded any of the Nereids—
"women's beauty" had become her least
favorite subject; and had her hands

not been tied, she would have acted
now with age-appropriate modesty
and covered her face.
Immobilized, she was still resourceful,
and filled her eyes with tears to stay
his impatience.

2

Rescue Mission: Code Name, Andromeda

Carlo Collodi would have relished that Perseus
didn't recognize his own erection and thought
some creature of the air must have—
but when?—stuck a javelin in his groin!
Ovid, swifter and more mischievous than
Sophocles, Virgil, or Lucretius,

packed a lot of action into lines
that go by in about—one-tenth of a second.
Mortified, he maintained air-space
as he hovered at eye level to his love—
with nothing, not even a backpack,
like any high school boy, to press

against his groin until his boner
subsided: never mind that her tears blurred
her vision, or that she couldn't think properly
until her rescue was secure.
Perseus stifled a laugh as the immense gap
between inner and outer worlds, opened,

and how until this precise moment in time
he'd lived his life on automatic pilot,
basking in the status the others conferred upon him
for performing tasks which they found terrifying
and he executed with such consummate
grace and ease he'd repressed his contempt

for these superstitious slackers
bearing stupid trophies and unctuous praise.
Like athletes and actors, the hero
performs in a realm set apart from the real,
where, when people die
they don't return for curtain calls.

That's why there are funerals.
You're looking for a myth of origin.
A truth that would survive transformations.
I don't want to criticize your Jewish
heritage, but prophecy—
Ezekiel's aphoristic thrust—

is not commensurate with poetry.
Jewish culture is—a survival code
for wanderers—still pre-dialectical.
Greek culture is advanced—
and Roman architecture has never
been equaled—.

Is there something in language that inclines
the mind toward imprecision—
because if you mean aqueducts,
funneling water from underground
streams and lakes,
it's inseparable from survival.

Yet in the service of a higher order.

3

Perseus' Bout of Altruism

Andromeda feared that he could take her silence
as an admission of guilt and chose to answer
Perseus' questions while pretending to ignore
their source in his personal interest in her.
The monster circled the shore,
groaning, churning the waters.

Her Mom and Dad, timorous as always,
clung to their immobilized daughter
as if they weren't why she was enchained.
Lacking dignity or pride, they cowered.
Perseus sensed they would have consented
to any request as long as he "took care of matters"

but feigned respect and asked politely
for her hand in return for "taking care of matters."
"Anything, anything," they replied in unison.
Perseus cringed: their pernicious
selfishness and cowardice was a far greater
threat to the future lovers than this "monster."

4

Consolation Constellation

The thought of all the horrible
transformations that occur in this book
in which she happens to be a character
petrifies Andromeda—momentarily torn
between the idea of a happier fate or
a more eventful life.

She offers a silent prayer that what happened
to Callisto when she laid her head down
on her quiver in the glade will not recur,
prays not to be raped by a trickster god,
scorned by Diana, or turned into a bear
by a rabidly jealous Juno

and threatened with death at spear-point
by her own long lost hunter-son
before Jove intervenes, calls a halt
to the horrible, stirs the whirlwinds and flips
Arcturus and the Bear upward
into the constellation room forever.

5

Flash Forward: Disbelief Suspended

Significant mythic figures were required to attend the Change Seminars. Centuries passed when characters remained alive in language only, limited to repeating actions that stayed the same except in reader's minds, or translations, or interpretations transplanted to other "disciplines"—shocking the classicists by digging up the bloody, painful clues to truths that once led men to blind themselves and women to murder their children. And who knows that these characters who exist only in language won't metamorphose into human beings, once technology catches up with imagination.

There's no need to explain why during the Renaissance Class the mythic figures burst into spontaneous applause. Though overcome with admiration for Marlowe's matchless versions of the *Amores*, they'd had trouble with lyric poetry because the scale was all too human and they couldn't see themselves reflected as transparently as in narratives like "Venus and Adonis."

They gradually overcame their initial antipathy to the novel (for its "lack of decisive structure") as they watched Miguel de Cervantes and Denis Diderot (without knowing that they had both, like Ovid, been the victim of the state's despotism, and spent time in prison) overthrow convention—what the reigning institutions designated as "art"—and adapt the necessary strategies to suit their age. Diderot's *Memoirs of a Nun* with its subtle yet dizzying transformations reflected through the heroine's character as well as the variety of convents to which she is dispatched only to undergo new travails just when the reader was sure the worst was over, struck a distinct chord and was judged one of the few works to meet Ovid's standard of cruelty—punishment far exceeding transgression, a government's corruption mediated through utterly debased "sacred" institutions.

But once novelists lost sight of the complex, perverse, unfathomable diagrammatics of the wish, and blamed an impersonal engine of society, they lost interest and were distressed and amazed that literature could become retrograde during a time when technological progress was making it possible for ordinary people, who weren't blessed with winged sandals like Perseus, to fly.

6

Distracting Transformations

Where is the beautiful aviatrix
with a plumb bob haircut in homage to Amelia?
I am pursued, as Perseus pursued Andromeda,
by electronic machines, devices that appear
to bring the world near but do something very different.
I'd rather be in desperate pursuit, like Perseus,
than chained to a cliff and subject to every
conceivable assault,
or surrounded by fax computer phone
whose signals jar, demanding answers,
taking time away from time.

7

A Question Arises . . .

The creators are dead forever.
Their creations are an open book.
Genre writers, look at Raymond Chandler or Ian
Fleming, invent characters who are ego-ideals,
as a way of overcoming their wounded narcissism—
who then take on an independent life.

Contra compensation, in *Irma Vep*
Maggie Cheung, fresh from a Hong Kong action flick,

plays herself—an actress laboring to become
her character, Irma Vep.

A veritable phantom, who never existed . . .

except to metamorphose in Feuillade's
seven-hour silent serial
Les Vampires.

How can she get inside the skin of a character who has no identity?

Whatever disguise Irma Vep assumes—
from the fashion plate outfitted
in a long tight-waisted skirt and tailored jacket,
to the perky sales rep,
to the nerd with the thick glasses and ratty overcoat—
she remains essentially who she is.

Always with her eye on the next victim.

You're way off track.

*I can't believe that that legendary what's her name,
the one who played the real Irma Vep . . .*

Jeanne Roques.

I can't believe that the real Irma Vep
could have looked as good as Maggie Cheung when—

as herself, remember, to delve further in the role—

she puts on that black latex body suit.

It's not the body in the suit,
it's the woman's ecstasy as she prowls
the hotel corridor like a cat burglar,
runs across the roofs of Paris in the thunderstorm,
stands on the edge, hurls the stolen
necklace into the night
to watch its glitter
rise.

And that wounded woman talking on the phone with no clothes on—
I thought Irma was going to bite her neck.
Instead she stole her necklace.

Irma is an agent for an underground
criminal organization.

Then why Les Vampires?

The title of the serial is misleading;
it's not meant to be mysterious.
Look at the shifting letters on the cabaret poster.

In Les Vampires *or* Irma Vep?

Either. Or better, both.

8

A Paradoxical Plant Is Born

Another minute chained to this cliff
and Andromeda vows she'll, she'll . . .
The sea-monster breaks water.
Perseus shoots upward.
The monster, mistaking his shadow
on the sea's surface for his body, goes after it.

Perseus dives, grips the creature's scales,
drives his sword to the hilt through his shoulder
blade. Not dead yet. The beast's
gracelessness and high-pitched squealing
incites the flyer to stab—with manic fervor;
yet with his last breath the serpent spews forth

a purple froth, drenching his pursuer's wings.
Perseus cannot wash off the gore
without doing something about the head.
The roughness of the sand demands he build
a soft mound out of underwater plants
before placing Medusa's head

face down. The soft stems stiffen, coral
is born, the nymphs know it and gather
at the site—and to get the go ahead to fashion
jewelry from this ravishing new substance,
they rush to adorn the terrible head
with sprigs and seaweed.

9

Flashback: Even Gods Can Be Jealous

If the thorny and pathless wood
hadn't been littered with stone corpses,
Perseus might never have made it
to the Gorgon's den, or broken through
to a new paradigm in Monster Slaying:
refraction, reflection.

It wasn't easy for a man used to wearing
winged sandals and whose element was air
to keep his footing on Atlas' concavities,
but he got as far as the camouflaged overhang
guarded by two witches who shared one eye—
which they passed back and forth.

Perseus studied this rhythm.
Then made his move.
Dove. Intercepted the eye.
Now he could see Medusa and avoid petrification.
Not a monster was stirring in the cave.
He steadied his shield, let Medusa's head

float into focus on the bright bronze,
then severed it. Looked away. Grabbed
the snaky locks and dropped it in a satchel.
He would always look away when he retrieved
the head to turn his enemies into stone.
He wondered if Medusa wondered

"What have I done to deserve this?"
A simple question eternity refuses to answer.
It was not her fault to have been born beautiful
or that her beauty was enhanced
by long, thick, lustrous hair.
What could she have done when Neptune

forced her down in Minerva's own temple?
The gods punish those mortals who reveal
any lack, any weakness in the gods.
Neptune's infidelity was a cover.
Minerva didn't give a fuck who Neptune fucked,
but found it so intolerable that a girl's hair

was more admired than her own
she turned Medusa's tresses into snakes.
Andromeda shivered at how easily
the powerful are threatened
and how close she had come . . . ,
and envisioned Ovid's own

FORTHCOMING

punishment: exile in Tomis.

(after Ovid)

II. DECEPTIVE PRACTICALITY

By metamorphosis, you mean
recasting that which appears to be
inviolable, static, fixed—

it's not as though you can change the street.
What is self-reflection in a world
that doesn't recognize itself.

I was torn between turning in at dawn
to hear the larks, or rising at dawn
to hear the larks.

My failed attempts to become
an early riser would make a modern
epic of repetition—the same

scene repeated with variations
that either supplant or amplify
the earlier action until no one is sure

which version to believe—
with one saving flaw:
no "epiphanies."

A history of defeat.
A man who cannot make life
easier for himself.

His idea of bliss? To wake in a downpour.
In a house in the woods.
Morning blending into night.

Water streaming on the glass
windows, doors and skylights,
streaks and blurs dissolving

the contours of the visible world . . .
Aficionado of obstacles,
he can find his way more easily

in the dark rain. She thinks he's still
attached to magical thinking.
He doesn't want her when it's "convenient,"

like any time before she's put on her eyeliner—
but the instant they enter the cloakroom,
the bed stacked high with furs,

he envisions that they could crawl
underneath, into the pitch
dark: she'd hike her skirt,

he'd pull down her tights,
(mid-thigh, no further);
they'd move without moving,

and be so still and quiet no one would know
they were under the already
humped mound.

Imprisoned by his fantasy, and suddenly desperate,
she mimicked that exasperated tone
women use to let men know the score.

"Whenever you're ready," she said.
He put his arms around her waist,
his mouth against her ear.

She stopped him in mid-whisper.
"And I'd be a mess!
I don't want to get undressed."

III. THE CHANGE SEMINARS

1

The luck of heroes, even those
who came to a bad end,
was to find a way to remain

unheard unseen
when their actions
weren't being recorded.

Heroes share a problem
with all performing artists—
how to deal with down time.

Whoever hasn't latched on
to a consuming hobby, or a sport,
or found a haven in family

life, the quotidian alone
is hardscrabble ground.
Now the couple's positions were reversed.

Andromeda would have admired
the attitude Andromache adopted toward
her heroic husband,

and thought it best not to let Perseus
know she knew he was not
unhappy, but floundering

in a delirium of inaction.
What luck to find a man who could
change, whose curiosity

knew no bounds, far outweighed
his male pride, and listened
to her with visible delight.

2

"I've been reading a book I think you'd like."

"Are either of us in it?"

"No, but he begins one of his best poems thinking of Andromache and moves on to you'll never guess who."

"Who? Orpheus?"

"No, a swan who rebukes the gods with every breath 'comme l'homme d'Ovide.' The book, *Fleurs de Mal*, was listed under fiction. I was going to return it but once I began . . ."

"Not the one who harnesses our stories in couplets!"

"No, that was Racine, the playwright. This is a modern lyric poet who has a lot in common with Ovid."

"I find that hard to . . ."

"Yes, yes, victims and exiles. There was one that blew me away. It begins with Andromache . . ."

"But she was real!"

(Silence.)

"More real than you or I, that's for sure."

"Are all mortals automatically more real than half-gods? Is Hector more 'real' than Achilles, and if so how could he kill him and drag his body through the dust as an object lesson."

"I'm getting confused with all these sliding categories. Go back to the poem."

"He's addressing Andromache while crossing a spanking new bridge, a trophy of the new order, over the Seine . . ."

"That's . . ."

"The river that flows under the bridges in Paris. But this is a Paris he hardly recognizes, though he knows the city as well as anyone since he's spent his life exploring the obscure passages alone, fencing for the elusive image. And on this sad auspicious morning he sees a swan who's escaped his cage, filthy and alone on the wet cobblestones, crying out for the cool, clear waters of his childhood lakes."

"Too bad they don't sound as good as they look."

"He thinks of Ovid exiled and the pitiful forms so many of his characters have to assume so that they can't even recognize themselves, when he realizes he too is exiled because his memories are lodged in places that have been torn down."

"So if he took some friends from out of town on a tour and every site he pointed out had been replaced they might think he'd gone mad."

"You're catching on."

"I'll read it when you're done."

"It isn't the kind of book you finish."

"Can I look?"

"There's more scribbling in the margins than there are words on the page!"

"It's in pencil, I'll . . ."

"No, we'll get two new copies and return one to the library. My treat. I'll bet if you turned those notes into a lecture you could wow the Change Seminars."

3

When it was Perseus' turn to speak at the next seminar his topic was "Baudelaire and Ovid: Two Forms of Exile." He knew that while no one would heckle the hero who turned Atlas into a mountain in an instant, it would still be a hard sell. To get his demanding audience to let down their guard he titled his lecture with a "self-evident point."

"Ovid Is An Anagram for Void"

"I was arrested by the emphasis
on boredom's yawning abyss.
Beyond resourcefulness.
The grimacing Frenchman prowled Paris
attracted and repelled but still
consumed
by worldly distractions—
crowds, gambling, exotic women—
and the fantastic conviction
that someday he'd overcome
all obstacles, not unlike . . . many who
are in this room right now.

Let us be grateful that
emptiness dawned on us long after
our legends were secure.

The author of *Fleurs de Mal*
reached his maturity in a world
where "progress" had become the rage:
no, not in the form of higher
spiritual development,
like his desire to find the unknown through the new,
but as mania for gadgets and machines,
anything faster had to be better,
like cutting time on a journey—
never mind what you might encounter on the way.
Efficiency was the key.
He vilified the salon's "official art"
and ran with the painters
who would be remembered:
Daumier, Courbet and Delacroix.

Later, an American cartoonist
would take Daumier's lead
and rig up the ultimate easy way
to shit, shower, shave, and dress
while pulleys delivered toast and coffee
to save what will always be their most
precious commodity: time.
(The files have been destroyed of those
mortals who rigged up facsimiles
and died from slit throats or electric shock.)
The sacred was endangered, as his once
familiar neighborhoods were torn down
and the streets he once strolled in comfort—
with the surety he might exchange a few
words with someone he knew, like the man he named
"the painter of modern life," Constantin Guy—
were history. Alone now with memories
no one else can verify he becomes
like a displaced person with a wild
look in his eye, like the king of a country
where it rains all the time
and neither courtesans nor the court
fool's malicious wit can cheer him up at all.
His spiritual exile, being internal, is almost

grimmer, because less tangible, than Ovid's.
The abyss grows wider.
I can see you're anxious to have the blanks
filled in to this stranger's self-estrangement,
but you know better than I that anything
worth thinking about takes time
to sink in. And Perseus has found
this more tiring than flying.
If you're dying to know what those on earth
have done with all the clock time
their inventions have allowed them to save,
Midas, not Perseus, is the one to ask."

4

Andromeda sat demurely on her hands.
She didn't mind that the others
would go wild over Delacroix
who brought stories alive for all time
with bold broad strokes
and a vivid array of colors,
sun-drenched yellows, rich Moroccan reds.

It might have been her time chained to the rock,
exposed to the elements, but for Andromeda
it was Courbet who painted the way toward hyperspace,
transformed matter into spirit.

There were so many questions afterwards that they scheduled another
session on the spot. Orpheus drew Perseus aside and whispered
"Baudelaire, helas!" "But do you think I offended Midas?" "No, every-
one knew you were speaking metaphorically and sensed you'd been
taken out of yourself." "Huh?" "Some power was speaking through
you. Remember Midas's lecture on Paracelsus?" "Oh yeah," Perseus
lied. "It's true I had to improvise because I couldn't find my notes,
but..."

Andromeda couldn't suppress a faint smile. Even though she was the
source of every idea Perseus had uttered her concern was focused on

how he had regained some self-esteem. He would be himself again. That was more important than getting proper credit.

Perseus touched her lightly on the shoulder. "You look like you're in a daze," he said. "Was I that bad? Why didn't you remind me about Midas's lecture on Paracelsus?" "You didn't tell me you were going to mention Midas. I don't think we even knew each other then." "What was it, another sermon about the dangers of greed?" "No, the Change Seminars are about going forward. And Paracelsus, who instead of using alchemy to change base metals into gold employed his powers to change the world. But what came as a revelation, especially to those of us who have also been transformed into constellations, was his belief that what's above is also below, that the galaxy and the body are one, and that the zodiac is branded in the body."

5

Transitions, while never easy, are vastly more difficult for mythical heroes whom people, more out of inertia than fixity, wanted to remember as they were—as in a cage of their own defining moments. Perseus told Andromeda that his dreams "went on and on," that it would take too long to recount them, that when he wakes up he still gropes for his curved sword. Andromeda thought: his mind is making up for all the mornings when he rose at first light.

Every morning, watching Andromeda rise
he was held captive by her beauty
while pretending not to have awakened.
He'd no idea why, if she saw him stare,
she'd throw on clothes, without a pause at the mirror,
go downstairs, boil water and manage
to appear so absorbed
in the raptures of sunrise over her book
he hadn't the courage to interrupt,
and be direct about what he wanted
or the subtlety to feign disinterest.
So he took his juice and coffee to the deck
and listened to the waves pulse
and throb, so that she would join him

and put her arm around his shoulder,
happy that they had in common
a love of silence, and grace,
and ultramarine distances without horizon.

POSITIONING IN TIME

Ah yes I was wrong.
Again I was wrong.
—"Lush Life," BILLY STRAYHORN

1

Spatial Interruption

Little common ground in the world we live in now.
The nature of generations?

It's more about getting back than getting beyond.
To the ineluctable fragments, the cryptic

propositions of logos, flux, and chaos.
It's more that our position in time puts us

at an angle to the real which severely limits
what we can know without our knowing it—

like the jetties erected to protect an eroding beach
alter the current far out on the ocean

throwing radar-equipped dolphins and whales off course—
and tosses a wrench into the elegant constructions,

blinds us like a ha-ha in such a way
that we're barred from knowing what it is,

blocked from seeing
by our position in time.

Prisoners of Function

Harder every year to assume a common ground;
every year, the earth—a lonelier place.

What if this is all, the beginning and the end,
right here, now, nowhere, in a place without charm.

What it broaches is the question of a road that does not exist.
Except a road that thinking throws down. Out of time.

There are those who are drowning and who
embark on oxymoronic quests with the least

amount of risk—all of their questions targeted
to annihilate ambiguous leads,

peril, detours, or plain old difficulty,
and so they hold back,

hold on to what they relied on in the past
to get them through with the fewest mistakes.

ON THE STRANGE LIVES AND UNTIMELY DEATHS OF
MARY URE, ROBERT SHAW, AND RICKY NELSON

> They are passing, posthaste, posthaste, the gliding years
> —to use a soul-rending Horation inflection. The years are
> passing, my dear, and presently nobody will know what
> you and I know.
> —VLADIMIR NABOKOV

> Cinema is the mythology of the twentieth century.
> —MICHAEL POWELL

1

The Age of "Who?": Famous Photograph

In Doris Lessing's autobiography she vents her anger at the media for coining the inapt phrase "angry young men," then locates one image to express the spirit of the era: "a famous photograph of the Royal Court people on some jaunt, on the top of a bus, lovely Mary Ure in front . . . every bit as fascinating as Marilyn Monroe, with the same fragility . . . her head back, laughing, but seems a bit panicky, from all the attention." As I plunged reluctantly further and further into a life I found disturbing for its lack of closure and abundant obscurity, I began to recoil from the "what are you working on" question and bristled when it was followed by the "but who is Mary Ure" question—and that's without getting into the consistent mispronunciation of her name.

Time will turn the tables; it's a matter of degree; here the reversal is complete. The beautiful pale woman who portrayed Clara Dawes in *Sons and Lovers* would never need a name, much less one as intriguing as Mary Ure. Having been a factor in a reverberant movement gave her an allure. I'd no inkling that the arc of her life and art was in any way complete by the time I saw her physically present on stage as Kate in the Pinter play two years before she would die. I don't know why I didn't say in *Old Times*, but have found that those who'd be loath to call *Cat on a Hot Tin Roof* or *Krapp's Last Tape* "the Williams play" or "the Beckett play," refer to a new play by Harold Pinter as "the Pinter play," the way they would an art show, or a performance piece.

When I saw Mary Ure physically present on stage, I was excited, susceptible to her fragile beauty, but my hair didn't stand on end as if I'd seen a phantom come to life. Here were husband and wife playing husband and wife. Robert Shaw, in civilian clothes, urbane, leavening his menacing persona as he delivered delicious lines that made us laugh—they were so close to the thoughtless banter that people employ so that they don't have to think. It brought me back: not to the familiar roles—they blended into one. If I mutter the syllables of his name, Shaw appears standing inside a garage with his hand on the flank of a gleaming Rolls or Bentley in *The Hireling*, about to burst the outsized silver buttons of his suffocating tacky gray chauffeur's uniform with the class anger and pent-up sex drive that was breaking his character apart.

2

There is no end to the torment that comes from watching dead actors
in old, and not so old, movies, and you always fall into the hole
of uncertainty; you know you don't know if they're alive or dead,
some of them look so radiant on films made not so long ago.
Richard Harris, the hero of *The Heroes of Telemark*,
is undergoing a second birth in old man roles,
while in the rockface rappelling, snow on castles
icecapade, *Where Eagles Dare*, two out of three leads,
Richard Burton and Mary Ure, are both quite dead,
as is her second husband, Robert Shaw.

A lot happens in *Eagles*, but what sticks
in my mind is the escape, where Mary Ure,
coifed, oblique glimmer of a smile,
cradling a machine gun
like a weightless toy on the caboose's deck,
bullets in mesmerizingly endless supply,
decorously mows down row on row of Nazi pursuers,

who drop into the white Alpine ridges,
like knocked over counters in a game,
as if she were answering the blasts

from Jimmy Porter's trumpet as they merge
with a shrieking train whistle and screech of brakes.

3

> To St Paul's Church, Covent Garden, for Robert Shaw's memorial service. A beautiful, still day. There was a gathering of figures from the profession, plus friends and family. Harold Pinter gave a short address, stressing Bob the writer . . . It was a fairly joyful occasion, serious but not sad. I had my usual bewilderment about our lack of ritual. We all huddled together in the sunshine outside the church—Paul Scofield, Kenneth Haigh, Harold, and many, many others. We all wanted to be together in Bob's memory. But what could we, un-Christian as most of us are, do? Off to the Riverside Studios to see The Changeling, beautifully staged by Peter Gill, precise and clear. But I had the impression of a not very talented cast dutifully following the conception of a quite brilliant director.
> —1978, Saturday 7 October, Peter Hall's Diaries

I abhor assumptions but from the tension Robert Shaw
emitted on screen and in his other incarnations,
the athletic boozer's fatal heart attack in middle-age
seemed at first less surprising than Mary's Ure's ambiguous end.

Shaw looks so painfully alive in *Jaws* as the shark-
crazed minor Ahab it's hard to digest
how quickly he raced toward a death
from natural causes, so shortly afterwards.

There's much that could be said about Robert Shaw,
a ubiquitous, menacing, explosive presence
during the previous decade in British films
before the American public began to pin a name

86

to the "intense athletic blond actor who played
Nazis and Custer, acted in Pinter plays, wrote
novels, such as *The Sun God,* and plays,
like *The Man in the Glass Booth.*"

He saw his marriage to Mary as "gloriously combative."
His comments to the press about *Jaws,* the novel?
"A piece of shit written by a committee."
Being married to this driven, indefatigable man

would have tried any woman's patience,
much less the Glasgow born, tough
but deep down fragile Mary Ure,
who no one dreamed would beat both Shaw

and Richard Burton to the grave,
choking on her own vomit after mixing
champagne and barbiturates.
The coroner waffled in his verdict,

claiming it "wasn't necessarily a fatal amount,
alcohol 208 mgs, barbiturate ratio 3.2. mgs in 100 mgs
though death *could* occur at those levels."
The *News* praised Mary's performance

for its "nicely judged mixture of the mystical
and the matter of fact," and lamented her long
absence from the stage. It was a review,
not an obit, and so no reason to mention

that for the past twelve years *Look Back in Anger*'s
original female lead, Alison, had been
otherwise occupied: giving birth to and caring
for four children. Champagne flowed

at the cast party and it was 3 A.M. before Mary
found her way back to the hotel room
in the West End she was sharing with her husband,
all wound up and wanting to talk.

Shaw wanted to share in her joy, but dawn
and his wakeup call for his final day of work
on "the regrettable *Diamonds*," was now
three hours away, "we'll celebrate tomorrow,

yes, tomorrow, darling, without the children."
She dosed herself, and took the couch in the sitting room
so she wouldn't be awakened when the phone

rang.

4

Regret

> What really killed her was the sudden release of tension and anx-
> iety. When she knew it was over and she was a success again, it
> proved too much for her. And she died.
> —ROBERT SHAW

Shaw sensed something, but had no reason to worry
about a woman who was used to taking care of herself,
their four children and the six from his two
prior marriages. And Mary,
who lived to live, and welcomed
the chaos of Robert's entourage
was an odd woman out in a field
where nearly every actor claims to be
"most alive when I'm someone else."

Shaw spent the rest of his life on earth
systematically breaking himself down
and died of a "*massive* heart attack"
four years after Mary's death.

This, her second marriage, was her first real
marriage and Robert Shaw retained his crush
on the tall, long-legged woman
with the light-blue eyes, seductive voice,
and flawless pale skin,
while continuing to fuck
whomever, wherever, whenever,
especially on Location Island.

She not only began in Mystery Plays,
she ended with her mystery intact.

5

Limited Run

I don't think I'd be haunted by Mary Ure's death
if she hadn't died so shortly after I saw her and Robert Shaw,
both looking vital, fit, and younger than their years,
play husband and wife in Pinter's *Old Times*
during a "limited run" in 1972 when I was scarcely out of college;
and if, in my raging resistance to time's eerie swiftness,
the event weren't wrongly fixed
in my memory as having occurred in 1982.

But there is no if in this: the triangle in *Old Times,*
the man, his wife, the other woman,
(the latter played by a darker blond, Blythe Danner)
recalled the earlier triad in *Look Back in Anger.*

I'm speculating that it was a limited run;
guessing that Mary, a mother of four young children,
aged from 10 to 2 at the time, would not have wanted
to stay in New York interminably. Or have I overlooked
what others would assume: that they would have brought
the children, put the older ones in school, and found
a nanny for the two little tikes, aged 5 and 2?

Such an obvious solution. I can't believe I didn't think of it
before I thought of it. Trying to ascertain the truth
hollows us out. Unless you'd rather take
your assumptions for the truth
and simplify the task.
The time to begin worrying
is when you think you're sure
of just about anything.

Not that facts require indenture:
an American obit I uncovered
noted that Rosemary Harris, not
Blythe Danner, played the wife's friend
but I will not relent.

I can see her entering, stage right,
as Robert Shaw rises for the first time from his chair
and Mary Ure remains seated,
back straight and perfectly still,
except when called on to cross
and uncross her legs,
in her white dress, cut

provocatively at the knee.

6

Again I Was Wrong

Why grab No Man's Land *and not* Old Times *off the shelf of the
Labyrinth bookstore, in the attempt to make your memory more real?*

Because *Old Times* sounded like a more appropriate vehicle for the old
guard's indefatigable knights, Sir John Gielgud and Sir Ralph (not
Tony!) Richardson, who had also appeared in a Pinter play on Broad-
way at around the same time—and it goes without saying that I
assumed that John and Ralph had been here before Mary and Robert.
And that I was wrong—though deep down I'm convinced that my
memory is more accurate than the dates of the New York runs
specified on the plays themselves.

*Just as you still see Blythe Danner and not Rosemary Harris in the role of
the old friend with whom the married couple reunites in* Old Times.

Who could hear the title *No Man's Land* and not think of Shaw if you'd
seen him scramble to hide from invisible enemies in Joseph Losey's
arid, paranoiac *Figures in a Landscape?*

No man. No nor woman neither . . .

And then there was that play of Shaw's that Pinter directed, *The Man
in the Glass Booth.*

You must have loved that.

Have never had any desire to see it.

I can't believe it.

It sounded both too claustrophobic and Kafkaesque for me.

But with *No Man's Land* the suggestion of
an inhospitable world

has the edge congenial to such
anxious and uneasy

presences as Mary and Robert,
to whom

uncertainty
had long been home.

7

The Luck We Didn't Know We Had

Shaw often said that both he and Mary
were "too smart" to be psychoanalyzed,
and yet he failed to recognize they'd escaped
a trap more deadly than the "shitty" action

films he resented having to do for money.
I'm referring to the set pieces,
the sententious adaptations of literary novels
with lachrymose soporific quasi-classical soundtracks,
where even the raindrops are charcoaled
to mirror the characters' invisible inner world,
the films derived from sources so renowned
they force otherwise fine directors,
into curbing their necessary perversity.

Alberto Moravia was luckier than many novelists
to have had Godard adapt *Contempt,*
and Bertolucci *The Conformist.*
And it was Brian Moore's luck to have *The Luck
of Ginger Coffey*—shot in a frigid Montreal winter,
and with great discomfort for the actors—
brought to severe life in black and white.
Robert and Mary played Irish immigrants
caught in a brutal economic and marital crisis.
It's an open question if either
gave themselves credit
for how good they'd been
in that low budget film.

It wasn't a blockbuster hit;
and hardly anyone saw it.

8

The Professional

While assumptions grow more out of thoughtlessness
than malice, they can blow up in your face.
Take what happened to Bogart on the set of *Sabrina.*
For twenty years he'd played physical parts,
his characters somewhere around 40.
His toupee, always a factor in this well-kept
illusion or screen image of an eternal early middle-age,
was useless, even as a talisman, when he was cast as

the older man in *Sabrina*, and the younger
star, William Holden, (not yet the actor he'd become
when more ravaged) was 35, blessed with thick
hair all his own, rugged good looks,
and taller and more muscular than Bogie had ever been,
and had the gall to ridicule the master.

In retrospect, if Bogie had known how ferociously
this golden boy had been hitting the bottle,
he might have been less easily inflamed.
But he didn't and, used to the camaraderie
on John Huston's sets, found himself again in a lonely
place, like the 12-year-old Humphrey
spurned and ridiculed by the other children.
Nobody would get the best of Bogie.
And that other William, Billy Wilder
would regret his numerous slights.
Desperate for revenge, Bogart spat curses
at that "filthy Prussian," "Kraut," "Nazi son of a bitch" . . .
Precisely the wrong tactics, as Bogie discovered
when he learned that Wilder,
despite his Teutonic accent—
which Bogie mimicked in front of the crew—
was a Viennese Jew
whose mother had died at Auschwitz.

Just before this misadventure the actor shot a *noir*
with Nicholas Ray, *In a Lonely Place*.
Bogart played the screenwriter Dixon Steele,
a man who, though sanguine most of the time,
and capable of great warmth toward those he loves,
is consumed with self-hatred for squandering
his flinty intelligence and fine education
adapting trash. Steele, given his waspy name
for a reason, lives on slow seethe: anger's vigil.
When roused—always for a good
reason—he is so quick to use his fists
that the cops make him prime
suspect in a murder case,
and the woman half his age

whose genuine love for him
is his redemption,
also breaks down—gives in
to the fear and suspicion
that destroys what they had between them,
leaving Steele where he began,
sealed now inside his bitterness.

While adapting the novel by Dorothy Hughes
the screenwriter, Edmond North, kept in mind
what he'd witnessed of Bogie's life over
twenty years: his awful marriages;
his bitter battles with studios.
At the time Bogie didn't let on if he noticed
that North filched details from his life
and used facsimiles of places he'd lived
and people he'd known.
"One of the actor's best roles," the critics wrote.
But the actor didn't like the film and never
looked back to see what they had seen in it.

9

A Dangerous Age

I've no desire to be so age specific but it's striking
that the script of *Old Times* calls for all three
characters to be in their early forties—

an ideal age for imaginary people—
when they stay the same age as the hero of a series,
like crime reporter Molly Cates, or

the raven-haired, blue-eyed, long-legged,
private detective of Seneca Indian descent,
Jane Whitefield, who can still run eight miles

through bush and brush in the dark when pursued . . .
though once again I have lapsed
into imprecision; Jane is the equivalent

of a Marlow, an Archer, or a Robicheaux,
but she isn't a detective. She's a guide
whose vocation is to help people disappear.

10

Why in the First Place

Maybe if I hadn't grown up hyper-aware
of my B-movie director uncle's grisly end
after twenty years in Hollywood and the 16 "B"s
under his belt I might not be
forced to think about these premature deaths
in mid-career (he was 44, Ure 42); and it's possible
that my reluctant interest has to do with an awareness of the many
who ride out the fickle and capricious wave,
the years when actors seem to disappear, and often
resurface. That is why I implore The Psyche-Professionals,
handing out antidepressants like Wellbutrin or Zoloft—
names coined to cast spells—in shovelfuls,
to devote some research $ to studying

                                 temperament,

how individuals are
inexorably, the way they are
barring corrosive and violent
interference.

It's possible that my uncle,
who landed in Hollywood right out of college
with a job—courtesy of his father's
primeval garment district bond with Jack
Warner—got his real break when he enlisted,

entered the European Theater as a commando
equipped with weapons, cameras, jeep, driver,
shot indelible stills on the Remagen Bridge,
and came out decorated for bravery.

11

Poolside II: Erratic Behavior

> "And now for Best Supporting Actress . . . the nominees
> are . . . Mary Ure, for *Sons and Lovers* . . ."
> —Hollywood, 1961, Academy Award Ceremony

(Poolside. Los Angeles. John Osborne and Tony Richardson sunk in deck chairs.)

The two men watch Mary walk drunk and naked out of their room,
hear the splash as she throws herself in the pool. Richardson, alarmed
by the silence, says she might have gone under. "Let her drown," was
Osborne's reply, before he offered Richardson another drink, at which
point the latter snapped his legs together, crossed the garden, and
returned with her in his arms. She must have fallen asleep in the water.
And would have drowned. Only when it was time for him to retire did
John see Mary curled up under a towel on the bed, fast asleep. The next
morning, awakened by her cheerful chirping, he fumbled toward the
bar to fix himself his day's first Bloody Mary. I was surprised that
Osborne refrained from skewering his wife on the pun that her gifts as
an actress were first noticed when at 16 she played the Virgin Mary at
the Mount School, York.

12

Direct Hit

Mary was also known for speaking her mind no matter what the con-
sequences. At a party in New York during the *Anger* period in the late
'fifties, the "butch" actor Robert Webber told John Osborne how she
defended his virtue, first by scorning a clumsy pass by Elia Kazan and

then—his male pride wounded—he taunted her by claiming "I hear your husband's a fag." She gave him "a good Yankee smack in his Armenian face, which turned her into an instant heroine, an exemplar of the fire-power of the frontierswoman."

13

The Tall Woman Appears

I glimpsed Mary Ure in *Sons and Lovers*
when I was still in elementary school.
It was the year before I was carted off
from an Illinois I had come to love
to a Utah I plotted to leave the moment
I was informed we would be moving there.
If I developed a crush on Mary,
it went underground until I saw her
dead presence alive
onscreen in *Where Eagles Dare.*

Tall, gentle, alluring,
she used minimal gestures
to express her evanescent
sexuality; distance; remoteness; mystery.

Mary appeared in the noncommittal
black and white, a luminous ghost
on the steaming railway platform,
even as her character, Clara Dawes,
disappeared from Paul Morel's life
after awakening his sexuality,
and turning his turbulent heart
away from mom.

Mary pale, almost diaphanous.
Her hair a whiter shade of blond.

14

Shadow Images

Actor's lives are different from all other lives.
And the screen adds an uneasy dimension.

A blurring of the real and the unreal.
The location and the set.

The question of *height* vis-à-vis the well-known cliché
about actors being short:

Alan Ladd on a ladder so he could talk eye to eye
with Maureen O'Hara or Joanne Dru.

15

Volcanic Changes in the Paradigm

I didn't know Ure was married to Shaw until I read her bio
in *Playbill* at the screening, scratch that, the showing, of *Old Times*,
or that she'd been married to John Osborne
while he torpedoed a soporific moldy archaic
post-martinis leisure-class closeted English
theater—opening the door
for the young and the bold
brooding throughout England and Wales,
Manchester, Birmingham, Dorset;
and the London Jew, Harold
Pinter, the tailor's son who decried
grandeur, rhetoric and spectacle,
and found the power inherent
in spare language, precise gestures,
repetition, and silences that allowed
the theater to fill with the sound of nylon
rustling, when a woman crosses
and uncrosses her legs in a tight skirt.

The English know what they like and the Coward
Rattigan crowd weren't about to pay
money to see thugs grunt monosyllables.
But no one would stop Joe Orton or Czech born
Tom Stoppard and once they climbed aboard
the English could at last reach across
the English Channel and shake hands
with the Irish and Romanian innovators
thriving in exile in Paris.

Now I've leapt ahead without making it clear
that John Osborne was everywhere
during the brief interlude
when new plays were labeled "pre or post *Anger*,"
with their shouts and kitchen sinks,
after which time I drew another enormous
BLANK about what Osborne had done between
Kennedy's assassination and his own demise other than
write his memoirs.

A friend exclaimed it was good he'd come through,
on the ground that a good book was a good
thing in itself. I muttered my tacit assent
and tried not to raise my voice in anger to explain
that an autobiography by an active playwright
and a man who never lacked the public's attention,
doesn't compensate for the plays
he would like to have written or at least
tried to write. A graph emerged
as I traced these abstracts from their lives,
and I hadn't expected to discover
that The Rise and Fall of Mary and John
ran strangely parallel in their mutual divagation
from what they had set out to become,
the initial role they felt destined to fulfill.

I'm sure the same thought is crossing your mind as it
crossed mine: that he and Mary Ure more or less
disappeared around the same time,
coming up for air to breathe
kindred disappointments
in different forms.

16

Inadmissible Evidence

Convoluted mistrust and entrapment.

The exquisitely tortured Nicol Williamson
taps harder and harder at the window pane
until it chatters, then cracks.

17

The Mist That Separates Us From the Things Themselves

Incipient melancholy. My own
I's disorientation in time's midst,
or "In a Mist," like Bix Beiderbecke's
hot music which I listen to on a CD
featuring the "real" Bix.

Time is like a thunderclap, and music
is like time in action. Paintings dissolve
the dimension of time.

Screen images stick in the mind.
Some of them become like Freudian
screen images that mask other traumas.

18

The Pretend and the Fake

Sam uses the words "pretend" and "fake" to
distinguish representations from real
things. Since all movie ratings are specious,
conflating the slangy use of curse words,
sickening violence, and kinky sex, I
risked taking him to whatever films I thought
would stimulate his imagination.

When I asked if he was scared, he'd answer
in a bold and firm voice: "No, dad, it was just
pretend." He found the distinction between
the representation and the real, absolute.

If anything in a film looks fake he'll let me know.
This usually opens the door to a dialogue on
what is objectively real and fake,
like locations as opposed to sets; or
scenes where an actor
appears to motorcycle through a town
as a bomb goes off and remains
fractionally ahead of the explosion
as smoke and flames fill the screen,

when the images were shot separately—
and the actor is riding in an empty room
where blocks hold the wheels in place and fans
blow his hair and the town is a model.
Invention hasn't kept pace
with special effects.

Since Sam's obsession with the real and the fake
runs curiously parallel to my own, and
since it's his responsibility to comment
each time he spots sleight-of-hand, cinematic
or otherwise, I asked if we couldn't

agree that all representations—all
art—and in this case screen images,
are equally fake, imaginary, "pretend."

The beauty of *Where Eagles Dare*,
and Mary Ure's role in it, beginning when,
a spy among spies, she's smuggled in
with the baggage in the belly of the plane,
is that it doesn't straddle the fence
of believability. Cast as the lone
female among rugged men
whose mission is to raid the German
stronghold in the frozen heights,
Mary bewitches the enemy in quieter ways;
extracts information with a glance.
And why break down the lovely moment
when she and her partner, Richard
Burton, reunite in an appointed barn,
which emanates warmth,
and Mary leans back against the haystacks
to welcome her lover's embrace.

So much had happened in
less than a decade,
who knows they hadn't rekindled
a fire that was lit when they played
opposite each other in the film
of *Look Back in Anger*.

19

The 'Real' "Custer," and in Cinerama Too

At last, another chance to work together, and in a film that had less chance of falling into the void due to a shoestring budget, like the luckless *Luck of Ginger Coffey*, despite fine work by author, actors, and director. The concept pleased Robert Shaw: two English actors playing the leads in a film about an American icon; a real man and wife in the roles of man and wife made it even more Brechtian.

And in Cinerama, and how could you lose?
And they'd be in Spain!

The place of choice to shoot an epic.

How could you lose?
The worst had already happened with *Cleopatra.*

And they could rent Orson Welles' villa, the Finche mi Gusto.

And there'd be enough room for their children and any of
Robert's who cared to drop in.

When their presence wasn't required on the set,
Robert would ride by day and write by night.
Mary loved to be in the sun: she would read, garden: be there.

Shaw thought the script contemptible, and rewrote it, line by line, to
make damn sure that this Custer film would be accurate and reveal the
parallels between the war against the Indians and the war in Vietnam.
Hadn't De Tocqueville demonstrated that it takes a foreigner to cast a
clear eye on America, a country so vast and young there's no bridge
between the crowd and the void?

Night, innumerable worlds showered down.
Sparks, ablaze, in swaying waves. A bonfire—
possibly set off and stoked by the actor
in a fit of drunken frustration—
consuming

props from *Citizen Kane,*
Welles' immense library of signed
first editions, and numerous raw
drafts from various works in progress
by Robert Shaw.

Typing paper is excellent kindling.
Mary awakened in time to get the children out
before the entire house caught fire
and blazed a trail across the dry
Spanish hills.

Come dawn, she and the children breathed
freely again, despite the odor of wet
ashes and the dust.

20

Long-Fingered Pianist

My mother changed her demeanor when she caught the scent of high
culture traversing the Rockies to reach Salt Lake City.
By the time she finished the Largo of her Van Cliburn
presentation, with exhibits culled from TV, *Time,* and *The Daily
    Bigamist,*
I determined to sulk my way through his recital
at the Mormon Tabernacle. His Einsteinian hair, dramatic
gestures, pauses, sweat and breathing—his pan-sensual
relationship to the piano—were far more noted
than the Chopin prelude he attacked in this acoustical
heaven (where you can literally hear a pin drop from front to back),
and I know my mother wasn't alone in too much explaining that
    Chopin
required long-fingered pianists. (My father's hands hung,
framed, on his wall, because an artist he knew
thought they were "beautiful, sensitive, expressive.")
All this fuss about hands made me dream of a dim, blurry,
black and white film, where the down and out heroes,
(the artistic temperament in a bad time),
are stymied, hungry and without a bed for the night
when the man (hunted, or a drifter) sees a poster,
and the woman walking beside him urges him to "try,"
swallow his pride and show up for an audition.

Interlude: Where's Beetlenut?

I don't think I knew anything about Tim Burton or *Beetlejuice,* I may have read a review, I can't remember, but I did now and then take Sam to the movies after his pre-k was over, beginning in dreary midweeks in late fall when the dark dank afternoon cold began to close the door on the day too early. The two of us entered the near empty theater in the middle of the movie and after we finished his popcorn and consumed some seltzer and Hi-C he moved over and sat on my lap. "Where's Beetlenut, where's Beetlenut juice?" This became a kind of chant that took on a cadence and beauty all its own as he said it over and over in his sweet, high-piping voice. "I don't know," I answered. "Are you happy?" "Yeah," he said, drawing out the word for all of its undercurrent of bliss. "Is that him, is that Beetlenut?" That was Michael Keaton all right, hairy, scary, and mighty small in his world that only the dead Geena Davis and Alec Baldwin could see because they too were ghosts. And except for Winona Ryder no one on screen could see them. "It must be Beetlejuice," I answered. "Good," he said, and we took it as a signal to have a long slurp of his drink. Then in an instant Beetlejuice had transformed himself into a giant neon green snake thrashing across the stairwell, at which point Sam's arms and legs went straight out into an almost perfect X and he popped up, appeared to hang suspended in the air, landed on my lap without a sound, and reached for his drink. "That scary snake scared me," he said. I was concerned that the snake had scared him too much, but no, he'd be fine as long as that scary snake didn't surprise him again. After that he hardly moved at all. He sat still on my lap while my eye was as much drawn to the way he looked, with his golden-blond hair in exquisite contrast with his blue OshKosh overalls, the nape of his neck acting as a kind of intermediary. All was silent and still and peaceful, cozy and warm. But he did lean forward when Winona Ryder "popped up" too, levitated rather, to demonstrate her allegiance to the ghosts, who were so much nicer than her own maniacal mother and whining father. We had escaped the hustle-bustle, the eternal chores, the barrage of phone calls, for a few hours. And he wanted to see the movie from the beginning as long as I promised to cover his eyes during the scary parts.

22

The Search for a Method

Beyond obits, reviews, and effusive
gossip from the glossies when John and Mary
were England's "golden couple,"

most of what I've otherwise uncovered
derives from a "celeb-biography"
about Robert Shaw that relates valuable

details while skimming only the surfaces
of lives, as if British readers would have forgotten
the subject before it reached the shelves . . .

As I try to fill in the enormous blanks
in my belief that there was nothing inevitable
about Mary Ure's demise,

my eccentric method of trying to understand
the unknown woman through her films
is subverted when none of Manhattan's semi-

archival video places carried any other
movies with her, not one!,
other than *Anger* and *Eagles*.

I'm brought up short. I can't conjecture
if Mary's tragic fate owes more
to native depression,
which led her to drink,
or her diminishing visibility as an actress,
which led her to drink more, or . . .

Uncompleted Lives leave me in distress
but who am I to say, or know?
I may be suicidal tomorrow.

23

Her Generation

By 1956, Mary had been feted by Binkie, fondled by Terry Rattigan, had
played Ophelia to Paul Scofield in Moscow, been featured on magazine
covers and appeared in two Arthur Miller plays. It was a fairly heady
début for a girl who had only intended to be a drama teacher in Glas-
gow. She treated the whole crowded sequence as if it had hardly taken
place.
                                —JOHN OSBORNE

Mary Ure had become widely known just slightly before such
    prodigious talents as

EileenAtkinsAlanBatesMichaelCaineZoeCaldwellJulieChristieTom
CourtenaySeanConneryJudiDenchDavidHemmingsAlbertFinney
ChristopherLoguePeterO'TooleVanessaRedgraveDianaRiggTerence
StampMaggieSmithRitaTushinghamDavidWarnerNicolWilliamson

all of whom are alive as the cosmos readies itself

and others who are still familiar to interested
parties while few people who came of age after
Mary Ure died have any idea that she lived.

Mary came from patrician stock
when her generation received a lot of press
for breaking through the class barrier,
wresting film and theater away from
the "good old boys."

24

The Killing Sweepstakes

Mary was the only actor
to receive bad notices in a Royal Court
production of *The Changeling* directed
by Tony Richardson. "Out of her depth,"
as her ex-husband phrased it, "in the midst of
all this Jacobean tooth and claw . . ."

Up to her death.

Mary never feared unsheathing her claws
when she was playing herself in real life,
but maybe at 24 she wasn't prepared
to be both angel and devil, the amoral,
murdering woman that Beatrice becomes.

Osborne's misogyny ran deep; he portrayed women in a beastly way.
There are many snapshots of Mary at her worst scattered throughout
his autobiography: "The bathroom was steaming, with trickling taps,
a trail of towels, sodden Kleenex, a wet stain of make-up and false eye-
lashes that looked like a laboratory experiment . . . The disorder and
sheer bloody mess Mary had left behind filled me with a feeling of
nauseous regret and failure."

Nakedness Her Shield

Beatrice: 'Tis time to die, when 'tis more shame to live.
—CHRISTOPHER MIDDLETON, *The Changeling*

And why should I, at twenty-two and in awe of her generation,
have suspected that the tall woman who had played her part in

Old Times with such fluidity and precision and made me listen
closely to every line she uttered through her subtle delivery,
was equally chaos incarnate the moment she stepped off-
stage, and had several times been found, during the play's

short run, walking around naked in front of startled stagehands,
and thirty blocks from the theater on Broadway,

or in Central Park at 3 A.M. in the cold of a New York winter
at a time in the city's history when most people would have wanted

to be armed as well as warmly dressed.
Just because, ten years prior, Mary had walked naked

from her room over burning sand out to the hotel pool
in Los Angeles and plunged in,

I saw no reason to assume she did this often.
I had no way of knowing that her drinking progressed

from naughtiness to an uncontrollable *dementia*.
And yet her actions begin to sound like axioms.

That when drunk, she took off her clothes.
That it was more of a problem at home than backstage.

Both marriages were battlegrounds.
Both husbands—worthy adversaries.

"Showing Up" Isn't 90% of It For Everyone

There are far more effective ways to die
than systematically drinking yourself to death,
impregnating your liver, and from what I'd gathered

from reports about Shaw's guilt-driven dark
metamorphosis after his wife's early and perhaps
unnecessary demise the night he left to shoot

the canceled scene in *Diamonds,* I expected a far
more bloated and less nimble Robert Shaw than the one
who showed up in *Force 10 from Navarone*

on AMC the other midnight, opposite Harrison Ford.
Was acting still a release, or did Shaw intuit
he would realize his goal and die at fifty-one

before this "latest trash" was released?
He was angrier than ever at his father,
who by taking his own life had left him alone,

with an unbearable burden and without a guide.
Force 10 is in the same "we'll beat the Nazis
on their own turf by adopting disguises" vein

as *Where Eagles Dare* and like Mary Ure,
he plays a triumphant character—not a Nazi.
A hero, not a traitor, not another dreaded "heavy" again.

(Would he have come to regard being cast
repeatedly as the hero as equally pernicious?)
And as he walks jauntily beside the younger Harrison,

fresh from his first star turn in the first *Star Wars*—
and about the age of Jesus when he took his medicine—
Robert doesn't look like a man who is fixing to die.

But appearance is not reality and the actor's
book was closed before *Force 10 from Navarone*
opened. "Big surprise," Robert would have shouted

over breakfast when it was crucified by the press
who go berserk over a dull action film and agreed that the sequel
had no "connection to the original *Guns* but in the name."

Shaw fulminated endlessly over "the shit"
he had to do "for the money"; yet "the money"
meant he could maintain a fleet of classic cars;

pay for the new Rolls; continue work on his private
golf course in progress; and cough up tuition
for "so many children he'd lost count."

His new humane agent tried to intervene and informed
the disconsolate actor that he didn't have to take
"this shitty part," because he didn't actually "need" the money.

He could, if he chose, go into his study and write.
He didn't have to squander his life. He could fulfill the frustrated
destiny "interrupted by this need for immense amounts of cash."

Was Shaw listening, or fixing drinks? He listened to advice
like his Ahabian alter-ego Quint listened to advice.
With deaf ears and a contemptuous malevolent leer.

27

The Fuse of Catastrophe

Films exist in an eternal
present, somewhere inside ourselves
we believe the lively, magnetic actors,
are still alive in real life,
that their strokes cancers and plane crashes
are the true hoaxes, that no one
understands. The night of the day after Ricky Nelson
died at 45 in that idiotic plane
crash

I had come home late, flipped on TBS
and noticed that *Rio Bravo* was on.
My shoulder bag fell to the floor.
I perched on the trunk that has remained in my life
since my childhood summers at camp
when Ricky's "Poor Little Fool" and "Hello Mary Lou"
and "Travelin' Man" climbed the charts
and melted our pre-teen hearts.

But now is not then and all the dead,
John Wayne, Walter Brennan, and now Ricky,
were gathered in the jail,
sitting nightwatch on a hostage
while Ricky and a freshly shaved and bathed
Dean Martin sang a duet
like a Greek chorus.

CHORUS

Strophe:
Dean Martin: Ridin' to Amarillo—

                        Antistrophe:
                        Ricky Nelson: ridin' to

Amarillo

                        Amarillo

Just my rifle, pony, and me.

Nelson: No more cows

                                   no more cows

to be ropin'

                                   to be ropin'

no more strays

                                   no more strays

will I see

Martin: round the bend

                                   round the bend

she'll be waitin'

                                   she'll be waitin'

for my rifle, pony, and me.

Then together: for my rifle, my pony, and me.

An "Ode to Solitude."

"Why don't you play somethin' I can sing with you," Walter Brennan
asks the two cool customers, and Ricky launches into a solo with the
refrain:

"Get along home Cindy Cindy
I'll marry you sometime."

I wept.

And Ricky, who spent his childhood and boyhood
in homes across America, and his youth on our 45's,
had died after many years in a mist
much self-reproach
drugs therapies

immeasurable.

28

No Quarter

Now the outnumbered heroes guarding the killer are dead,
while on screen, in another scene that will remain
the same forever—sinister trumpets

in a variation of "Deguello," played by Santa Ana's men
at the Alamo—penetrate the cell.
Shivering the spine.

But it was heartening that Dean Martin was still alive,
and by 1985 he'd not yet abandoned
his daily round or his eye for women.

He took his time disappearing
though as the end approached
he was loath to do more than watch

old Westerns on video, alone. Even golf,
the game his so-called friends testified
he lived for more than anything on earth—

"the sort of contact Dean liked,"
clubface and ball meeting
for a brief 450 millionths of a second—

no longer held its once sustaining magic.
I saw a similar depression hit my father,
who when he ran into a wall of dead desire,

wouldn't even take a call from his oldest and closest
friend. Letting go of all that binds you to life
is a full time occupation, although I doubt

he let go of his loathing for that "no talent bum,"
Dino, as if detestation were desperation's last
claim on existence itself.

(The mind fixates for a reason,
but that reason is often obscure
and lacks the glue of logic. Probably

Dean Martin reminded my father of
a successful version of himself.
Or something like that.)

Rio Bravo employed
a formulaic plot and familiar actors,

but Hawks twisted the focus to show
how Dean Martin's "Dude,"

a down at the heels drunkard,
consumed with self-pity since he lost

the woman he loved,
regains his dignity.

29

Who is more vulnerable to mayhem than men
on the road, with a rock n' roll band, crew,
private plane, funky pilot.
If her husband and his wife had entered
the room in time, Mary Ure and Malcolm Lowry might have been
saved. Ricky Nelson had kicked the habit,
but cocaine was thought to be a factor
in the fire; he could control himself
but not his band; or the pilot—?

Invisible demons love to ambush the reformed.

Who would have imagined that Ricky Nelson
would die before Dean Martin?

In "The Garden Party," a song he'd set down some fifteen years before his death, Nelson addressed a rock n' roll scene that had changed beyond recognition and, in taking stock, appeared to have caught himself before beginning to tailspin.

Would that were the case.

30

Death by Misadventure

Before I found out that Mary died in 1974 instead of 1982,
I fantasized that if Mary and Ricky had met they might
have talked about falling, about being less in demand
at forty than in their mid-twenties.
Unarguably out of step.

Known but superfluous.

They might have compared the pitfalls.
The mood-swings.
The war between the desire to cope and the desire to throw it all away.
I cadged that phrase "Death by Misadventure"
from the coroner's report on Malcolm
Lowry. The same mixture led to an end
the same as Mary's: each choked on their own
vomit. *(Pause.)* For the record I wrote "moment"
in the hardbacked 6 x 9 green National® Record
ACCOUNT BOOK I take with me wherever
I go. It's invaluable in a world
where the right hard surface is hard to find,
and we're forced to work like *plein-air* painters
without the easel, or mountains that stand still,

pull out bound books in taxis and on steps,
in subways and on streets, ready to be visited
when we're thinking *groceries*.

The moment is more accurate than the fact.
Past and future intersect.

It could be said that each "choked on their moment."

Mary loved her children, but what did love mean?
This universal problem whose nature
is to be in flux presents special problems
to the actor, for whom the real doesn't exist
unless they're working, secured in a role

which demands above all
that they be someone else.

Transformation is the key.

Mary and Ricky were both ticketed for a coroner's report of
Death by Misadventure.
Catastrophe's fuse was lit.

Never mind overdoses. Alcohol and barbiturates
were Mary's well-tried method for winding down—

one morning she would wake refreshed!
To a new beginning.

BICOASTAL: BOBBY DARIN AT THE COPA

for my fathers

In the summer of my sixteenth year, my stepfather
got a pulpit in Beverly Hills he would have loved
to have been permanent: Rabbi to the stars.
We rented a furnished pad on Sunset Strip
where many an afternoon it was the singer Jack
Jones and me alone at the pool,
only Jack's deck chair was surrounded
by an entourage: agents, managers, vocal coaches,
toupees, gold chains, Hawaiian shirts,
who yakked and gesticulated with cigars as batons
about his current gig at the Coconut Grove,
analyzing his previous night's performance
for what should be kept, what dropped;
and I thought what a good singer he was—

("though not as good," both the fathers agreed,
"as his father, Allan Jones, the tenor")—
but that onstage he lacked the personal touch
of Bobby Darin at the Copa when he stepped down
and mingled among the audience and sang "Dream
Lover" to a golden-haired little girl
who would have been in kindergarten,
and asked in a tender and intimate voice
"How old are you darlin'?"
and "Is the room too smoky for you?"
My father'd consented to take me to see
Darin at the Copa, because he'd read that the kid
could really sing unlike the others
he considered goons with pompadours
who depended on echo chambers and tricks.

"THE SECRETARY OF LIQUOR"

(JOHN F. KENNEDY'S INFORMAL APPOINTMENT OF DEAN MARTIN TO HIS CABINET)

> What the fuck did they want, these men who needed the
> company of others to make a life, as he needed a woman
> to make babies?
> —*Dino*, NICK TOSCHES

> I always plays to de common folk.
> —DEAN MARTIN

1

It was casting time for *The Young Lions.*
Brando wouldn't hesitate given this chance to dye
his hair white and do a German

accent. And while no one would hire Monty Clift
after his facially disfiguring car-wreck,
Brando convinced the studio that the other, slightly

older, kid from Omaha was the right man.
No one could play a more sensitive-tough than Monty,
like the artist-bugler-boxer Prewitt

mistaken for the enemy, gunned down
by his own men in the Pearl Harbor dawn;
or the way, as the seraphic cowboy Matt Dunson,

he got a rise out of his demented empire builder
father, John Wayne, by kicking over a tin cup,
sloshing the coffee into the dust to show his disgust.

Clift knew that *Lions* director Edward Dmytryk
was searching for someone to play a key
supporting role—as Frank Sinatra had in *From Here To*

Eternity—yet he was stunned to hear it was
"Jerry Lewis's partner in shlock."
Clift softened, nauseated when he saw

Martin's competition
pander to the crowd on Broadway.
Lucky for Monty that he let it go: the two men

not only became friends; it was Dean
who put the man with the wired-jaw to bed
when he had the chloral hydrate and alcohol wobblies.

Ignorant of Brando's intervention on his behalf,
Monty told Dean that Marlon's fifty takes per scene
were getting on his nerves more and more

and he vowed to walk off the set if he tried
ONE MORE TIME to have his German soldier die
with arms spread wide to "echo the crucifixion."

Clift, wasted with self-recrimination at forty-five.
Martin, an actor for whom one run through a scene
almost always sufficed.

Dean got a chuckle out of Monty with his response.
"It should be awful good with so many takes."
Then the future flashed before him.

"I guess there are directors who want us to do
the same scene over and over again too."
"Sure, lots. Some of the best."

"I guess I got spoiled. Jerry and I got
to where we pretty much called the shots."
And then—without any foreknowledge

that he'd be doing his only two other
serious roles in the next two years
and be subject to directorial rule on the sets of

Some Came Running and *Rio Bravo*—
he vowed in the future to set up his golf net
before shooting started on a picture.

Dean appeared to float, perfection
never an aspiration: that he was already as well known
for his insouciance and drunk persona as for

his singing and acting doesn't mean he was so well-defended
that he didn't feel any pressure about working
with such aces as Brando and Clift.

He didn't have to stretch to play a would-be draft dodger,
Michael Whiteacre: "a likeable coward like myself,"
a screenwriter in Shaw's novel, a singer in the movie.

The army doctor feeds Dean his first line in *Lions*
as if his future were visible in the instant:
art and life exquisitely commingled.

Doctor: "For a man your age and in your profession
you're in excellent health. How do you manage it?"
Martin doesn't hesitate: "Clean liquor."

But sauntering through this role didn't mean
everything was swell: he felt so out-of-place
on location in France he gave up the offer of

a choice part in *The Guns of Navarone*
because it meant going back to Europe.
In his middle years, he ambled through the role

of "Matt Helm" in another toneless
Bondian takeoff, and when Columbia
wanted to shoot *Murderers' Row*

on location in Cannes, Dino
set the studio straight: "fuck no,
just build some fake Riviera sets."

2

A diffident crooner, he needed a stooge.
License to fuck around on stage.
After his split with Jerry, Dino's drunk persona grew

into a ghostly partner, and by the time he had his own TV show
the public was so saturated with his presence,
many conflated the persona and the person.

When he landed the drunk's key role in *Rio Bravo,*
he turned to Brando for help, "what should I do?"
Brando told him what to think about.

The more inscrutable the subject
the more this spectre stands out in relief.
Part of Martin's appeal was that no one knew him.

It wasn't a mask; his detachment was who he was.
He showed up, his spirit remained elsewhere.
His wives and children found him unknowable.

It wasn't personal. When the Martins entertained,
the guests carried on while Dino disappeared
into his room to watch westerns on TV, alone.

It wasn't personal. When the producer of
"The Colgate Comedy Hour" suggested they have lunch
to get to know one another better, Dino

set him straight: "No one gets to know me."
Martin was a man no one came close to knowing.
What does it mean, to know someone?

3

Why ask such questions at all after Socrates
beguiled us out of answers and set us on
the inexhaustible path . . . dialectics?

Do you think I haven't wondered if I haven't
strayed from my true path as I find myself
tracking the trajectory of such non-exemplary lives?

You're thinking it's a trick, and will not answer,
but before you judge my dissolute subject—
who liked the money but thought all the attention

was a joke because "a singer is nothing"—
as a derelict choice, consider how philosophy,
while striving to become more concrete

continues to recoil before the problem of other minds.
And it is said that Monsieur Sartre turned paler
than his martini, when Raymond Aron

challenged the Husserlians, at the Bec de Gaz
in Montparnasse, to make philosophy
out of a cocktail glass.

4

There's something about everyone no one can know.
There was no question of Dino taking orders
and being bossed around was out of bounds:

penalty shot incurred for the perpetrator,
who was, this time, the imperious Billy Wilder
whose streak of hits was breaking fast.

Dino as always was doing his job,
which was to literally play himself in *Kiss Me,
Stupid*, and Billy had the balls

to cap an interview at the Hollywood Press Club
with this tactless pearl: "stars don't mean a thing."
Was this because of what *Stupid* might have been

had Marilyn, whose presence he had counted on,
not done herself in? Was Wilder gambling
that fellow exiles from the Reich,

Lang, von Stroheim, and even the ghosts
of Lubitsch, Brecht and Thomas Mann
would have been there to applaud and acknowledge

that he, from a younger generation of German exiles,
was one of them?
Dino didn't brood. Dino didn't blow.

There would be no humiliating histrionics.
He would put Wilder in his place
with a letter, denouncing him as an arrogant

and self-important son-of-a-bitch.
Without angling for the director's respect,
he got it, and more.

After six weeks of delectable footage
with Peter Sellers—whose American debut
was to have been in *Stupid* —

as the small town piano teacher
intent on writing a hit song
and enlisting Dino to "get it in the right hands"

the tetchy "thirty-nine year old actor had a massive
coronary," yet not long after landing in Heathrow
found the breath to bitch to the press

about crowds on the set, wrote a letter
vilifying Wilder and Hollywood,
and swore never to return.

Wilder was used to being the abuser, not the abused.
He had to take it out on someone and no one better
to bark at than Sellers' replacement,

Ray Walston, as they reshot scenes.
Ray was cowed. Dino knew it.
Ray observed that Dino was never without a glass

in hand but assumed (wrongly) that it was filled
with ginger ale instead of vodka.
Which Dino was this, the persona or the person?

Dino advised Ray, IN A VOICE LOUD ENOUGH
SO THAT EVERYONE ON THE SET COULD HEAR
to "tell that cocksucker to go fuck himself and do it your own way."

Wilder went wild. Martin practiced putting.
"If you wanted an actor, what the fuck did you get me for.
Why didn't you go get fucking Marlon Brando."

It was as if Dino, who'd boxed in his youth
under the pseudonym "Kid Crochet,"
had sucker-punched the dictator, who found himself

disarmed by this unflappable and far from ugly,
American. Dino's aplomb had Wilder
on the floor, howling with laughter, just as night-

club audiences used to crack up
out of sheer anticipation of the antics to come
while waiting for Martin and Lewis

to begin their act . . . which knew no limits.
They didn't break rules, they made them up
as they went along, as when they leapt from the stage

followed by floodlights in Fort Lee, New Jersey,
to chase a slender tall brunette in a white dress
down the aisle, chanting, in imitation moron—

"we know where you're going, we know where you're going"—
because she had the nerve to leave her seat
before they'd finished their act.

She was mortified, but not for long.
They had no way of knowing that a young
woman who was that well put together

could be as painfully self-conscious
as this anonymous girl, who within a few
years would become my mother.

5

There is something beautiful and horrible
about Dino's incarnation of cool.
Anger sublimated into a mask

that would not harden, could not crack.
Dino did not end in ruin, like the others.
His falling away was gradual.

His lifelong withdrawal, prelude to silence.
Henry Miller had finally gotten *Tropic of Cancer*
through the courts. He'd spent his life

in quest of freer spirits than his own,
and now, after Rimbaud and Lawrence
and The Colossus of Maroussi,

he found in Martin a priest of irreverence
who was beyond nihilism,
who shrugged off everything the doom culture

deemed valuable, and pulled strings to be
granted an audience with the man
who made heavy weather of nothing.

6

Driving home to the suburbs during rush hour
in the huge gas-guzzling cars that signified
America's boom economy in the 1960's,

married men without time sighed for the first
time all day when "Houston" came on the A.M.
Then, back in their gaudy palaces at last,

they stacked Martin's LP's
on the turntable while mixing martinis.
Was it the facade that never cracked, never changed guises?

And isn't facade precisely the wrong term for one man's
unchanging way of being in the world?
Dean would say that's it's a waste to waste this wasted

unasked for sojourn on earth thinking about shit
like what others think of us, or depressing shit,
like "the fucking Cold War or Vietnam,"

or rip-off artists like the Beatles
("why do they spell it with an 'a'?").
Jealous? Never. Only annoyed that they kept bugging him

with questions. Why did he have to think?
Wasn't it enough just to live? Dino didn't work
to see his voice or image reproduced;

he acted, sang, and hosted shows, on screen
and in person, because it was easier than real
work.

Dino liked his inflated wages, but money
meant nothing beyond what it could buy.
"A singer is nothing." Why did he sing?

It was the easiest way to make a bundle.
When anyone complained that acting was hard work
Dino responded as Crocetti, the barber's son

from Steubenville: "You think acting's work?
Try standing on your feet
twelve hours a day dealing Blackjack."

7

If you agree that Dino lived to live on his own terms,
and if his triumphs were in the significant films
where he had allowed himself to take

direction, listen, learn, tremble and transcend,
then his second greatest trope
after inventing himself

was convincing producers and directors
to let him play a character
who sang and drank and thought about golf more than god,

so that the actor and the part were entirely one.
His string of walk-through roles
was like a continuous aside

to his audience, dissolving the boundary
between actor and spectator
and giving birth to a suspect and shadowy intimacy.

MONEY

for John Berger

Until this grisly season
of forced good cheer, I had come
to my fortieth year with-

out thinking of money
as more than something to buy
time with, enables its possessors

to go on and do what they
deem most important to get
done before our cruelly

limited life-span drives home
its final . . . tour-de-
force . . . The season is—

the season. Gluttony frees everyone
to lapse into silence or
indulge in banter so impersonal

those with the least
to say—flourish—as lights
enhance the winter trees.

Then this Christmas
card arrived, postmarked from the town
where my wife spent her teens.

I took one look and looked away.
And left it on top of the pile.
She came in, took one look,

and said o*h my god.*
It was something about what the card
signified. Money

joined hands with philosophy:
the card moved us somewhere
beyond language; her

exclamation was homage to being
wordless in the world.
I didn't dare calculate the cost

of having the children's
portraits painted and then
photographed for the card.

Looking at the triptych
from left to right a figure emerges:
the older you become the more

power and confidence you will
have. I don't think I have
progressed beyond

the panel on the left:
the hesitant expression
of the youngest child

beside a storm-colored urn.
Not even the portrait artist
can disguise the slight

rigidity in his posture,
the way his arms do not
dangle freely but conform

only outwardly to the pose
that has been chosen
for him—as if he were

saying here, *take my
shell, I'll hold on
to my soul, thank*

you—or am I too much
projecting my way
of keeping myself to myself

when as a child someone *I*
hadn't authorized was looking at me
with a design, or about

to shoot my picture
and the timing was off
and I wanted to be

elsewhere: out
of my body.
My wife's long hair fell over the mail.

A Christmas card sent
in all innocence. With the best
intentions! I put my arm

around her waist, my hand
on her hip (—I knew how hard
she was taking the triptych—)

while we greeted each
other in the dark foyer, her
winter coat—still—on her back . . .

TWO HORATIAN PALIMPSESTS

I. HIDDEN CLAUSES IN THE LOTTERY YOU
CAN ENTER FOR FREE

All my life I feel I've been walking steeply uphill,
the simplest acts immensely difficult,
       from putting on a shirt to changing a tire,
          to say nothing of irritation,

as when you've been put on hold and your neck
begins to cramp and then it's dial tone time
       and again you're forced
          to begin again.

If everyday life pretzeled everyone
I doubt the species could have come this far.
       And you, Delius, couldn't have lived
          so many lives—would-be

assassin, traitor, ambassador, double-agent, go-between,
pornographer, procurer—without keeping your head.
       Marc Antony might never have set
          eyes on Cleopatra had you—

circus-rider of civil war—not handled the reservations.
When others would have hidden, you rode where you had to ride.
       And Horace wasn't feigning surprise
          when, on one of his

rare trips into Rome, he heard an ode recited so well
it mesmerized the crowd in the silent piazza:
       "when things are going your way
          do not let your joy

transmogrify into a manic high, because—
whether you're sluggish or indefatigable,
       whether living means problem-solving or
          lounging on a grassy knoll

in summer, sipping the Falerno that matured
during your absence—you will die."
          It sounded familiar—didn't he once labor
              for just this,

lines imbued with a rhythm rooted in Greek choral meters
that lashed his Latin into a faster dance?
          There's something to be said for questions.
              Have you ever

asked yourself why the tallest trees, like umbrella pines
and white poplars, caress branches, throw shadows
          on the ground? Have you noticed how silently
              the river courses

toward the open sea? If not, don't fret. But when you find
yourself descending into a dry river basin
          where the bottom's caked and the stones
              are as hot as

burning coals, you've found a worry worth the worry.
The general consensus holds: America is a young
          civilization. But why do the young
              take this to mean

that never letting go of the Net is the door to the future?
Never assume. Quarry fresh ideas from the ancient world
          where the workers still have long lunchbreaks
              and wine.

And let no picnic go without roses about to open;
so long as no one on earth can stop the Three
          Sisters from reeling in the inexorable
              black threads

while death's hired gun, Orcus (the shadow that "had to be
an illusion"), not one to play favorites between
          the man with old money and the one
              without prospects,

makes his move—one more *domani* and he'll cut your throat—.
It's time to decide who will inherit the yield of your life's
        quest, the vast empty desert acres
            you bought for a song;

your Virtual Reality equipped loft in Soho; your hilltop house
in Tivoli, where the slate-gray Hudson gleamed
        metallic through the trees in the light,
            when you could still bring

your horse to drink and then, naked, ride him bareback
as the fish brushed deliciously against your skin.
        I will wipe the smirk off death's face
            until it ceases

to presume we're all too weary to rebel against our fate
once our souls have crept into the shaken urn until our lot falls
        and some glassine figure stuffs
            a one-way

ticket in our hand   to board the   foul   vaporetto   to set out
on this   free
        perpetual   exile   junket.
            Like hell we are.

                                      (after Horace, Odes, II.3)

Amigo, my heart leapt when I beheld you.
It's been so long when, side by side, we said "no!"
        to surrendering where others would have seen
           an endgame situation.

Pompey, initial comrade, in whose company,
time and time again, I have overcome the rank
        quotidian, civil war's yawning tedium
           with dialectics and wine—

(but not before I gave my hair a sheen with the moisturizing-
fixative cream endorsed by the stars—who emerge
        from death-scrapes with each strand in place),
           and now that divided and dividing man,

Brutus, has given you back your citizen-
ship, beneath our variegated skies.
        A favor: When you see your parents, convey my praise
           for their having named you after

a city built under a volcano: risk at your fingertips.
Our assassin-leaders had to witness 24,000 die
        on the first day alone at Philippi
           before the thought first flashed: suicide.

The crown is always seeking new heads to settle on.
What choice had I, having misplaced my shield,
        but to stand by as the other side
           made our men bite the dust.

I was beginning to tremble when Mercury carried me
through the enemy lines in a heavy mist.
        Invisibility is a kind of answer
           but it remains

divinely indifferent to our wills. Did any god intervene
when the undertow sucked you back and back
　　　　into the iron world of swords?
　　　　　　　　It's hard to forgive those

who didn't throw you a line when you needed one
but now that you've returned alive after the brutal
　　　　battles you endured, don't deny Jove his promised feast.
　　　　　　　　Your long campaign done,

lay your body down beneath my laurel tree,
fill the shining goblets we have filled in your honor
　　　　and drink. This Centerba Forte is what
　　　　　　　　they would have given Christ

on the cross—instead of that potent but sour water
and vinegar mixed with wine—had it existed then.
　　　　And if you are at all enchanted
　　　　　　　　by the abundant phials, choose

whichever scent you like to pour into the night air.
Venus R.S.V.P'd that she'd "attend because she knows
　　　　that" our "crowd, like herself, also loves
　　　　　　　　throwing the dice."

I'm eager to hang one on, like the wildest of
The Wild Ones, for it is not every day when a friend
　　　　given up for lost is somehow,
　　　　　　　　miraculously, washed ashore.

(after Horace, Odes, II. 7)

THE COUPLE

1

The woman stands on tiptoe to kiss the man and for a moment,
with their twin-teal backpacks, parkas, and other gear—
they look like one new creature. A mutation.

2

Seated in *La Rosita* their gear guards the table
where they sip *cafe con leche* and lean forward,
sitting tall, pelvises tilted forward,
to talk—whisper?—their physical closeness
almost embarrassing (but to whom?) at this early hour—
light rivering in her chestnut hair,
their foreheads almost touching as they sit
further forward straddling their chairs
toes pressed down, heels up, wrists crossed;

a posture almost too intimate for a public space
at breakfast but somehow right in the Spanish café.

She says that while it is absurd to sell forsythia
it is a small miracle to buy cactus
on 107th Street and Broadway.

(If they're strangers in Manhattan
they seem more at home than I've ever been.)

They listen to the brisk chatter and clatter of plates
and music from the Spanish station
which now plays "Yellow Submarine"—
universal language?—"our friends are all aboard."
They study the menu and note
the beautiful sounds
words like *huevos* and *arroz*
make for eggs and rice. The generous

syllabic count and vowel length
seem like an echo for their love. And their desire
to linger. (Other eyes
are on them, not only mine.)

They have drawn
the morning from a sea
of newsprint—in at least three
languages—toward their window seat.

3

The light changes along with the brisk pace of the walkers.
Someone in a tan Mackintosh reaches out to hail
a yellow cab, while the sun gilds
the fire escapes and people rise
energetically from their beds.

4

Don't their eyes tire of each other?
Or is it not the eyes that tire?
They're not looking, they're drinking,
communicating through their skin
several inches apart.

Love can't be trusted.
But that doesn't mean it isn't real.

They linger over coffee; he strokes
the back of her neck; she doesn't feel
impelled to look up or stop but, later,
she kisses him behind the ear.

And in the mountains there is
snow melting to get down from the heights
to pour through the clefts in the twisted
rocks: natural arches, obstacles—horseshoe shapes.

And in the plains there is
a dropping of the shoulder-armor,
a tingling in the hip sockets, so that even a chance touch
at the hipbone startles the center and starts
a slow convulsion—

release of two creatures
(peculiarly, perilously at odds),
used to training their gaze
on the peripheries, like this
bicycle tethered to a parking meter,
orange handlebars, silver trunk like a treasure chest
perched—not locked—on a wrought iron ledge
fixed over the chrome wheel-casings—
blue shadow-dappled twig-littered canopies,
or the small tantalizing cursive *c*
in the blue neon soft as silk, announcing

> *café Equense*

where the couple might return in the voluptuous dark.

The dark, quietly vibrating like a Mouth Harp,
or her—noiseless—breathing . . . or,
when they are lost in Olmsted's
misty, labyrinthine rambles
and, framed by traffic, they pause
beside the lake in the dank air
where the water is still,

> another
world from the blood-running pavement,
the meat-packing plants

gray and dour below the rotting piers—
warped—(and will they be replaced
with fresh wood or fazed out with poured
concrete that knows no give or take—no—swelling—...?)

What can love repair?
By what force of love
can they imagine themselves beyond
the squalor that surrounds them
onto another plane
blessed and blessing!

6

Who invented ecstasy?
What man or woman
first walked around
with its burden?

Cold shelter from the street,
among the bronze
mailboxes, inside the bright red—
freshly painted—door jambs.

He picks her up under the buttocks,
she arches her thighs around his hips,
plants her feet on the tiles:
tongues firm, yet tentative,
learning their own momentum;
(the rubbery wall of her mouth
takes him further in and in.)

Tongue and tongue, freckle and freckle,
tears, shuddering, swelling
in the places where they used to ache,
"ain't no cure,"
knowing this touch,

this grave flicking
of tongues could never
be repeated, or knowing
it *could*—

knowing it in another consciousness.

7

He strokes her neck at the junction
where the occipital bone and cervical spine
cross, engage, spark;
coccyx tingles, cock rises toward
her, not into her, through her, to her;
rises as he plies
the inside of her ass and thighs,
or rubs the crevice where her right
forefinger and thumb divide,
stroking her cheek, or the hollow below her earlobe,
ankle bone, clavicle,

tonguing every millimeter,

until sea dissolves into sky

(their raft turns over
in warm water and they are that water,
and bob, afloat, buoyant;
at rest in secret knowledge of each other's darknesses . . .
        and now he could weep.)

But there is no ice in the water where they would roil and tumble,
and where avenues welcome those who walk hand in hand,
gait easy, backpacks half-full,
half empty—
the sun coming out now, as if synchronized to their desire—
and as the runners circle the reservoir
they lower their eyes to adjust to the light

bouncing off the water to ignite
the cinders; the green through the dead-
ice capped leaves;
a small curve, an indent on the track
gleams like a bracelet,
before an azure haze takes over.

8

It gets warm. She has to peel her Anorak.
She cups her hand over her eyes
in the light and wind off the reservoir,
to see the easy arcs the gulls make as they spiral upward
over the all-angle roller coaster of the rooftops,

in the comforting thud of other feet,
as if lulled by the sound of a lover's heartbeat;
                        danger, in
distraction; she must kick the chain-link fence in order to set
off again, get back into the stream, put her mind back into her body;
        her body: slender; deceptive.
There is a power in it she has always known. And feared.
Or feared others would fear.
But it's difficult, with others, always—just how to say it?

Necessary to hold some one thing back.
Whom could she trust to let it out?
It might scare her. (Scare him.)

9

Dawn, a smudge of charcoal, lifted by noon
and his body, as if heliotropic,
was drawn toward the flares of lilacs,
and now he knew to move cautiously,
keeping his eyes on the ground to not,
as he has done several times, catch his foot on
a stone or root cluster and fly off, gashed.

10

He's relieved when night comes on.
He doesn't need his eyes to know
swallows congregate on the stark, bare limbs.
The darkness grows through the darkness
of that winter tree.
Soon they will be one
and no one will see them.

ELSEWHERE

Before sleep last night I lay there in a reverie
over LA, and dreamt of it all night and put off
getting up for fear it would go away.
All my fears of flying dissipated at the thought
of cruising in the air to Los Angeles.
I was happy there. I said (in my dream) to M.,
"I know it's too late to go anywhere"—we had arrived at dusk—
"but let's take a spin through Beverly Hills anyway."
My eyes hurt. I thought a drive through the quiet green
world of Beverly Hills would be a cure.
And I was back in the silence of the receding houses
broken only by the ticking of sprinklers.
Paradise was a rugged garden compared to this.
And then I thought, "No, I'd rather seek out my cousin
in the Korean restaurant above the bookstore near UCLA."
The part of me watching the dream thought
But your cousin is no longer there. She was never there.
So it wasn't my cousin. It was a phantom.
So what. I wanted to go. It was no phantom.
It was a girl named Beverly from Burbank
from whom I mysteriously drifted away.
Gray-eyed, olive-skinned, mindful,
she wore horn-rimmed glasses even at fifteen.
But the quality of the light at the end of the street—
the ineradicable smog-tinge that almost made
the sumptuous plush excruciation
of the sunset more bearable, like the fumes
hovering in the clement evening and the flow
of traffic down Laurel Canyon from the valley
to the sea, the people getting out of their cars to chat while waiting
for the light to change, for the traffic to move,
the horns as if scored by Gershwin,
and I remembered the letter I received yesterday
from a friend who was on his way
to LA, and what could be better than to be
in LA when it is winter here,
and the predictions are so dire

I cannot listen to the weather or the threats
of war. My mother tells me I loved
flying as a child. "But," I wanted to yell
out of sleep, "it's because we were flying
to LA. I liked the people there.
They were happy. They didn't quarrel so much."
Now those same people may be gone or dead
but that sunny mood must have something to do with the place.
I envy my friend's journey and sojourn there.
I can see myself, in Malibu, draw the drapes
of a glass house on stilts as the dawn slides from gray
to honey and feel my dread ebb away
as the breakers make their way up the beach.
And it seems useless to go anywhere, to do more
than stand in the motel lot, in the sulfurous haze,
one hand on my suitcase, the other still
slamming the door of the rented car.

VOLTERRA

There's a dark side to the light in Volterra.
It's nothing like the brutal, capsizing, pulverizing stare
on the sun-blinded streets of Marseille, and you're free

to scramble through low tunnels that form
a maze of their own and must have concussed
many an unwary attacker.

I arrived just in time to watch shutters close, shops darken.
Stark streets, hard and harsh walls.
Nothing like it in the world.

It sounded like it could bite, Volterra.
It sounded like what it was:
a remote, fortified city in the heights.

The drawback—not the labor of hauling
provisions up those steep cliffs,
but something more impalpable: stasis.

At midday this unsparing, sunless glare,
releases the pain in the basalt, an ancient pain,
preserved in the twisted torsos and anguished expressions

of the Etruscan couple on a sarcophagus lid.
Places do this, when they're unmasked.
Reveal their history in an instant.

It was out of kilter, Volterra, tilted.
A woman's head, gigantic, pre-perspective, grotesque,
leans out of a second story window, disapproving.

Familiar German appliances sparkle in the windows of the shops.
My mood began to go down.
There was so much pain.

Every step forward brought
more fortress, more isolation.
But Etruscan, not Roman.

An improvisation. Not a system.
Volterra, isolated from the other Etruscan cities
even before the Romans—the real

barbarians—broke through the gate
and brought the future to Volterra.
But the Volterrans couldn't take the time away

from living life to acquire Roman know-how.
There was always the chance of exuberance,
the dance, and what came after.

The sun in our faces as we walk down
the decline to the scarcely marked tombs,
dark moldy caves filled with nothing—

except lidless sarcophagi platforms and lizards,
quick, alert, maybe grateful for the company.
It's a bleak place, this ruined ruin, sightless site,

whose treasures are set among other
inestimable plunder, in the Villa Guilia or Volterra's own
Guarnacci museum.

I walk many times this distance in Bologna or Rome
without my legs turning to stone.
This wasn't the soreness of other excesses.

(—Mere fun compared to how *Voltaren*
burns like an acetylene torch
through the stomach linings of the living.)

But the almost unspeakable quiet of siesta
is like metal brushes on drumskin or cymbals.
A yellow sign points toward the cliffs:

the shadows under the cypresses and pines.
What relief to breathe easily for a while in the heights,
beneath the desert flower—broom—

resilient, firm, and strong though rooted in arid soil and cinders
like the crater of Vesuvius;
so beautiful when its blossoms are in flame.

My eye rises from the cool vaults of a cracked
cathedral on a hill to the Apennines, to the Alps.
Ringed with towers, like Montereggione,

a delight in itself to see, Volterra is not.
But it is fronted by a tercet of Etruscan heads.
We exit through the gate at twilight, gentle, serene, and look up.

Three heads, triangular, at the top.
Muddy brown. Features effaced by weather.
Twenty-five hundred years of weather.

A millisecond, an hour, a day.
I looked a long time at these heads,
I don't know why, my spirit revived,

I was lighter happier, I hugged my wife,
I could feel the life return to her body too.
Who is not, deep down, Volterran?

There is still what happened.
In this corner of the world
where a little of my spirit

holds itself distantly.

Notes

LONG-STEMMED ROSE

In Section 5 of the poem the dialogue with Shakespeare's plays is both overt and oblique. With "What, moody?" the spectral inquisitor adopts the language and tone of Prospero to Ariel. "Longèd long" is a phrase—notably awkward and difficult to pronounce—that Ophelia uses when she returns "remembrances" to Hamlet (III, i).

THE SHALLOWNESS OF THE LAKE

I seized upon this title to stand in opposition to the traditional use of a lake as symbolic of depth, a repository of mysteries. It has none of the "stilled legendary depth" "as deep as England" as the pond in Ted Hughes's early poem "Pike." The real Great Salt Lake is also famously shallow. It is also where Robert Smithson, in *The Spiral Jetty*, which was underwater at a time that I made a pilgrimage there but has since resurfaced, hypothesized that the structure of the salt crystal was the structure of the cosmos in miniature.

FRAGILE CRAFT

My friend Katharine Washburn, whose sudden and untimely death occurred not long after her great Norton anthology, *World Poetry*, was published, was the primary reader of several of these poems. We had collaborated on a translation of Euripides' *Daughters of Troy*, and her expertise with regard to how to adapt classics became legendary as she guided poets toward the kind of poetic versions she wanted for the anthology. She had a tremendous capacity for empathy, the kind that could foresee what you didn't know you needed until she fed you the seed of suggestion. Katharine also liked to play the role of Svengali with a number of her close friends in more apparently casual ways too. One winter we were talking about our favorite escapist films; she insisted that I had to see *Where Eagles Dare*. But while it seems unimaginable that watching an adventure movie to chill out would lead me into a long poem that meditates on the peculiar form of immortality granted screen actors, I wonder if there wasn't an element of magic in her lighthearted recommendation. I wouldn't put it past Katharine to have wanted to guide me toward a new site of inspiration.

In Section 1 I quote part of this passage of Doris Lessing from *Walking in the Shade*: "There is a famous photograph of the Royal Court people on some jaunt, on the top of a bus, lovely Mary Ure in front—she was every bit as fascinating as Marilyn Monroe, with the same fragility. The young lions and lionesses are laughing, and every young lion, and most particularly John Osborne (who would shortly marry her) and Tony Richardson, is watching Mary, who has her head back, laughing, but seems a bit panicky, from all the attention."

When writing Sections 17 and 18, I had in mind this remark of Alfred Hitchcock: "The camera is not photographing the screen and what's on it; it is photographing light in certain colors; therefore, the camera lens must be level and in line with the projector lens . . . . But I did the most dangerous thing I've ever done on that picture and I'll never, never do it again. When the little man crawled underneath the moving carousel—*that* was actual. If he had raised his head an inch, two inches—finish. My hands sweat now when I think of it— what a dreadful chance I took."

In Section 28 the bugle call played in *Rio Bravo* is "Deguello." It means give "no quarter." Take no survivors.

Unless otherwise cited, the quotes pertaining to Mary Ure are from John Osborne's autobiography, *Almost a Gentleman*. The details of Robert Shaw's life are from John French's biography *The Price of Fame*.

" THE SECRETARY OF LIQUOR "

I am indebted to Nick Tosches's splendid biography, *Dino*, for some of the details from which I have fashioned this meditation.

TWO HORATIAN PALIMPSESTS

Odes, II.3

These poems are a continuation of work that appears in *The Millennium Hotel* and *Provoked in Venice*. In "Hidden Clauses in the Lottery You Can Enter for Free" the phrase "circus-rider of civil war" is a translation of "desultorem bellorum civilium," Mesalla Corvinus's epithet for Delius. Horace's "Delius Ode," as it is often called, sets the groundwork for the double, triple, and quadruple agents who appear in modern spy novels.

I have rendered Horace in the third person here. Once he acquired his spectacular farm in Tivoli he hated to leave it. In my poem Horace has wandered into a square in Rome where he admires a poem he hears being recited, and doesn't recognize that he had written it.

Odes, II.7

It is clear that Horace dropped out of the melee at the battle of Philippi, though I'm not sure how literally to take his lines about dropping his shield and fleeing. This is a deft allusion to the then well-known poem by Archilochus that ends:

> It was a beautiful shield.
> I know where I can buy another,
> Exactly like it, just as round.
>
> —ARCHILOCHOUS
> 78, tr. Guy Davenport

ABOUT THE AUTHOR

Mark Rudman is Adjunct Professor at New York University and recently received fellowships from the National Endowment of the Arts and the Guggenheim Foundation. His many books include four from Wesleyan: *Provoked in Venice* (1999), *Realm of Unknowing* (1995), *Rider* (1994), and *Millennium Hotel* (1996).

WITHDRAWN
FROM COLLECTION

LIBRARY OF CONGRESS CATALOGING-IN-PUBLICATION DATA

Rudman, Mark.
The couple / Mark Rudman.
   p.   cm. — (Wesleyan poetry)
ISBN 0-8195-6577-6 (cloth : alk. paper) —
ISBN 0-8195-6578-4 (pbk. : alk. paper)
I. Title. II. Series.
PS3568.U329 C68 2002
811'.54—dc21   2002006947

THE TECHNICAL COMMUNITY COLLEGE

3 3063 00111704 2

DATE DUE

9-20-03			
GAYLORD			PRINTED IN U.S.A.